Dog Behaviour Matters

Sara Whittaker

First Edition

First printed in the United Kingdom

Published by Whittaker Publishing

Paperback ISBN-13: 978-1-9168726-2-2
eBook ISBN-13: 978-1-9168726-3-9

Whittaker Publishing
5 Harold Street
Leicester LE2 8AL

Dog Behaviour Matters

SARA WHITTAKER

CONTENTS

Chapter Two – Indoor Toilet Trouble

Chapter Three – Being Noisy

Chapter Eight – Phobias and Other Weird Stuff

Chapter Nine – Reactive / Aggressive Dogs

INTRODUCTION

I've always had dogs - right from being a baby. They have been a central part of our family and featured heavily in all our activities. We were lucky back then, the dogs we had were easy going and slotted into our lives without a ripple. I've had some 'horrors' since and have had to painstakingly pick through one issue after another. It hasn't always been easy, but it has been worthwhile. Whilst I have had a few simple issues with the pups I have raised - mainly during their adolescence - the bigger problems have surfaced with the 'second-hand' dogs I've acquired. Not all from rescue centres as you might think, the worst offenders have landed in my lap from more innocent quarters. The Dog School client who's work situation has changed so can no longer keep the dog. The behaviour consultation where the owner handed me the dog and said, 'You have him' ...and actually meant it. The owner who religiously brought her dog to classes for the first year but simply had too many young children to properly care for her. So many of them.

Dog Behaviour Matters is the latest instalment of my updated version of Think Pet! which was published in 2005. The first half is 'Dog and Puppy Matters' which is a birth to death guide. This new instalment is all about problem behaviour and practical ways to work through it.

I've been working full time teaching dog training classes

and behaviour therapy since 1998 and I've developed many concepts and techniques which are tried and tested and are now available to you in this guidebook. There are many different approaches to what seemingly 'is the same problem', and this is to be expected as no two dogs are the same, nor are families carbon copies of each other. There are personalities involved and previous experiences to factor in along with breed differences to deliberate and levels of training for both dog and human to contemplate. Hence, there is a wealth of crossover of problems and solutions and what improves one dog's behaviour may worsen another's. Just to give you a little insight into why behaviour therapy can be very confusing and contradictory.

There are a few things to be said about behaviour therapy. The first is you can't fix it all at once. It takes time, consistency (which is absolutely key), and patience above all else. Good days will be followed by horrendous days and then again by good days – until the good days are all that's left. This can take many weeks and months. The second is, and this is particularly true if you have many issues, to pick your battles. Make a list and work on the bits that irk you the most. Trying to do everything at once may make you disappear up your own backside! Thirdly, explore basic training and simple measures before you go for stronger, more complex solutions and lastly, try not to blame the dog, yourself, or anyone else that's had dealings with the beastie. It really doesn't help.

I have tried to give an explanation throughout the book as to reasons why a dog might be doing 'what it does' and in many cases proffer different approaches for each. So, all I can say now is enjoy the read, think through the issues, and above all else – don't forget to enjoy your dog…!

SARA WHITTAKER

Sara Whittaker has worked as a leading Pet Behaviour Therapist and Dog Trainer for over 20 years. She owns an established business, WitsEnd® in Leicester, which offers help with behaviour problems in both dogs and cats, training courses 6 days a week, and boasts a physiotherapy and hydrotherapy centre.

Sara was also an external Lecturer at The College of Animal Welfare® for many years where she taught students, the general public, pet professionals and Veterinarians on a range of subjects including dog and cat behaviour issues, setting up puppy parties or classes, aggression problems and dealing with common behaviour matters. In the past she has taken part in TV and radio, but she now prefers to focus her time directly on clients and their needs.

Sara has two grown up children, and a husband, who is a Veterinary Physiotherapist, and she currently has four dogs; Strumpet the Pug aka stinky food addict, Parsnip the needy Springer, Cricket the gorgeous (and knows it) Sproodle, and Pancake the crazy Cockapoo.

Dog and Puppy Matters... and *Dog Behaviour Matters...* are a revised and updated version of *Think Pet!*, which was published in February 2005. *Dog Behaviour Matters* contains some excerpts from *Dog and Puppy Matters.*

CHAPTER ONE

Where to Begin

1.1 The Impact on You

Behaviour issues with a dog can be hard to live with. Even minor challenges can snowball in our mind and become much more than they really are. They can weigh us down and force us to rethink each activity on any given day to avoid specific situations or places, even certain people and their dogs. Unchecked, a problem dog can create daily stresses for their families and drive personal anxieties, mowing down an owner's self-confidence and eroding relationships in its destructive path. But you still need to trust your instincts. You still know your dog and still know more than you think. Deep down, *you still* know *your* dog well. As a dog owner, you know when he is unhappy or stressed. You know how he is feeling most of the time – or do you?

Problem behaviour is typically driven by emotion and more often than not the things our dogs do are fuelled by feelings of reward. Not necessarily the expectation of a treat or in the form of praise from us, more often it comes from the emotion they feel on doing something specific. Take barking for instance. The feedback they get from repetitive barking relieves anxiety, making a dog feel better. Likewise, running away from a thunderclap brings about a euphoric barrage of 'I've survived', and all the heady feelings that evokes. Bouncing about crazily on the lead at another dog can bring a colossal adrenaline rush leaving said beastie giddy with the tidal wave of emotions. Put simply, its often nothing to do with us and everything to do with how the dog feels and what he gets out of behaving in a particular way.

So, taking this into account, stressing about our dogs embarrassing interactions or mortifying indiscretions doesn't help. Losing your confidence to walk the dog again serves precisely zero purpose. Blaming yourself for every wrong move a dog makes is a path to self-destruction. Tackling the problem head on - consistently, patiently and with well thought through knowledge - can make life with a dog enjoyable once more.

1.2 It's Not Just You

Dogs are very different to us, and at the same time very similar. So why is it you think your concerns regarding your dog are exclusive to you? As a fellow dog trainer says to many of her clients, 'Don't feel special, this happens a lot'. A good number of dog owners share the same queries; some trivial, some considerable. We can all experience 'situations' from time to time that we feel we can't cope with on our own and reach out for help from professionals or through guides such as this. Often asking other dog walkers if they know how to 'fix it'. What you must remember is, what works for Peter who lives in the next street, may not work for you and your dog as you are both individuals with your own unique personalities and household settings. So, having tried Peter's sworn-by technique and failed miserably, don't blame him, or worse, don't blame yourself – try something else.

1.3 The Dominant Dog

We have been conditioned to feel a bit guilty about having a special relationship with our dogs. Many clients have said, in countless behaviour consultations, that they allow their dog onto the sofa, or that it sleeps in the bed with them. "I know it's wrong" they whisper guiltily. What is surely wrong, is for people to feel bad about something that is so good. Your relationship with your dog is very personal – as is mine. We share our homes and our lives with them. And how we choose to live with them is an individual decision.

Do we need to dominate our dog? Do we need to dominate anything or anyone that lives with us? In my opinion the answer is no. Why invite a dog to live with you, and then try to control his every move? What we need is a strong relationship, built on good communication, trust and love. We have to understand our dogs' needs and try to fulfil them. We can teach him with clear, consistent signals how we want him to behave in differing situations. By sticking to simple ground rules, we can educate our dogs to do what is expected of them, quickly and without confusion.

Do our dogs need to dominate us? In my view the answer is again no. Dominance is controlling behaviour. When a dog is labelled as 'dominant' it means he either believes he controls, or is trying to control, the family, house and garden – aiming for status of 'top dog'. This makes him sound more like a terrorist, planning a coup in the house!

Dogs are naturally opportunistic; they will take every opportunity to bring themselves pleasure. This can sometimes make them appear manipulative and self-centred, but hey! It is the nature of the beast. Some experts suggest we impose rigorous conditions on dogs to avoid them controlling us and to ensure we control them. Strict rules are designed to 'take the dog down a peg or two', and include such things as removing all their toys, feeding them after we have eaten, sitting in their beds to show them who's boss, and ignoring them when they seek our attention. What we really have to ask is, what do these rules mean to our dog and how much of this approach is really necessary?

Excessive discipline directly affects our dogs' general happiness. Their emotions will vary from mild insecurity because their owners aren't taking any notice of them, to heightened anxiety because the rules are simply too much for an animal to cope with. They might feel intense frustration at having all their pleasures removed. Imagine how you would feel if you no longer had access to things, people or activities you enjoyed; you'd be depressed, angry frustrated, miserable, and stressed!

In some households, changes in the dog's emotional state could be deemed a success – for instance the very lively, over-bearing attention seeker suddenly becomes sullen and quiet when all his pleasures are taken away. The question we have to ask ourselves are:

- Is this really a long-term effect, or will he eventually seek rewards in other ways?
- Has he learned to behave differently, or is he simply feeling differently about his circumstances?
- Is this really a success for the animal?
- *Do I really want to live with my dog like this???*

Many dogs, especially those that cause problems for their owners, are too easily labelled as dominant. I have had cases referred to me as dominance problems, when in fact the animals were frightened, nervous, hyperactive – anything but controlling. Their emotional response was perhaps linked to previous learning or a current situation. When a behaviour pattern is explained in terms of the dog's emotional behaviour – how he thinks and feels – often the dog's 'parent' can find his or her own answer to the problem. Through proper understanding, a solution often shines through.

Our dogs do try to manipulate us, not because they are born 'control freaks', but because they are essentially selfish in nature and want what is rewarding to them. We need to firstly accept this, and then look closely at how we deal with it.

It is important to consider what the dominance theory can do to the nurturing relationship, the emotional bond that develops between dog and owner. If the owner has removed most of the reasons for having the dog in the first place – something to look after, companionship, shared experiences, and mutual affection – the dog may no longer trust his owner and perhaps view him with suspicion. The majority of dog owners I have met are uncomfortable with the dominance concept, but they may not have been offered an alternative view.

Sheba was a two-year-old German Shepherd female referred to me for 'dominant-aggressive' problems towards her owners. But she was only aggressive to 'Mum and Dad'; with their two-year-old son Jack, Sheba was a perfect angel. She was calm around him, never murmured when he pulled her hair or tweaked her ears, and even acted as his walking aid when he took his first steps. She had never bitten, choosing rather to growl menacingly at her owners in specific situations, like when they sent her to bed or tried to get her to do anything such as sit. Sheba would allow Jack to play mischievously with her food, but if his parents so much as looked in her direction when she was eating, she would grumble.

Having taken professional advice, Sheba's owners were told she was dominant (which they already knew as they had read all the books) and was trying to rule the house. They were advised she needed to be brought back into line. Certain strict rules were to be instigated immediately, such as taking all Sheba's toys away and only allowing her to have them when her owners said so. Sheba was not fed until her owners had eaten. Her access around the property was to be restricted to the kitchen and garden only, and she was not to have contact with Jack as she was 'too dangerous'. Sheba was put on a choke chain when walking and was schooled to obey instantly every command given, by force if necessary.

Sheba became more aggressive within a few days of these changes. One of the reasons she got worse was not having contact with Jack, the one person in the house who didn't threaten her. Instead, he played with her and gave her love, affection and pleasure. Sheba was aggressive to her 'Mum and Dad' because most of her interaction with them had been negative – shouting, forcing her into bed and removing her food. She simply felt threatened by her owners, who incidentally loved her dearly. What a mess!

Her owners felt terribly let down. They had, after all, followed all the rules from day one of owning Sheba as a young puppy. They'd read all the books, had trainers to the house, as well as taking her to classes. They had come to the conclusion that she had been born bad and nothing would change her. It took just a bit of explaining how Sheba was feeling – threatened and insecure, with no real pleasure in her life – for the penny to drop. Once they understood the basic principle that 'dogs have feelings too' we began to make alterations to their daily lives to ensure Sheba had regular 'fixes of pleasure' – games, toys, training using food treats and of course contact with her beloved Jack. Simply fitting a head collar (see 10.7) to Sheba made it possible for 'Mum' to take her to the park every day with Jack in his buggy, something she had previously not been able to do, as Sheba pulled and choked herself on the chain.

Training Sheba to go to her bed willingly was easy. We just had to motivate her to want to do it, or rather to do it happily and not feel punished by it. Putting a special toy stuffed with treats in her bed did the trick, changing her perception of the bed from punitive to rewarding. The food aggression problem was side-stepped by throwing out the food bowl that she had been 'taught' to guard and replacing it with a food dispensing toy that she could roll around and feed herself from (see 1.17). But the biggest difference came from the owners' change in attitude. Released from the rigid regime of always ensuring Sheba didn't become 'top dog', they felt free and able to communicate with her as a valued and much-loved member of the family.

1.4 Status Reducing Method – Not Recommended

Popularly known as a Rank Reduction Programme. I've worked with dogs with behavioural issues since 1997 and still have yet to meet a dominant dog. Here is a list of the methods here that are commonly used to reduce a dogs' 'status' – with my take on what the dog might think is happening.

a. You must walk in front of your dog or he will think he is leading the pack to go hunting.

This assumes that the pack leader is always the fastest chaser in the hunt, however the pack leader in most social groups is typically the best communicator. And taking your dog for a walk in most cases is not a hunting situation! Dogs pull on the lead because they want to get to where they are going faster; it becomes a habit – simple.

b. Ignore your dog if he approaches for attention.

This is designed to make the dog feel insecure and not get pushy, but in reality, it can start to undermine your relationship as the dog may feel you are unapproachable. However, it does depend on the method employed to get your attention! Avid attention seekers will employ a myriad of approaches to get your attention, and these should be ignored. Likewise ignoring your dog while he is resting is not a punishment – it's just common sense. Trust is hard earned and easily lost, and this is one way to go about eroding it. Some dogs could feel punished or that they are in trouble and become anxious. Ignoring any social creature is quite a severe punishment, as you will no doubt understand if you have ever been 'sent to Coventry'.

c. Ignoring your dog when you get home.

Ignoring your dog's attentions when you get home will probably make him try harder (jump harder, nip at clothing etc.) to get your attention (see 10.11). Some dogs will feel upset (as in point b), which could start separation type problems – toileting or chewing when left because the manner of the owner, when returning home, upsets the dog. I can't think of worse than getting home and my dog not even getting out of his bed to greet me. There's something a little unnatural about this rule. Obviously, you don't want the dog going mad, so you need to keep everything low key.

d. Take all the dog's toys away and only let him have one when you say - so you control them.

Dogs like to play with toys and if there are none, they will play with whatever is available, a mobile phone, slippers or a nice stuffed cushion. Those canines who are not into toys simply won't notice what you have done except the house is tidier!

e. Feed the dog after you have eaten.

This is one of the 'wolf pack' theories. The leader always eats first – but does he? If a dog eats immediately after you (which is the only way he is going to know somethings up - see 1.5 and 1.13) then he may start drooling in anticipation.

This is not something a dog has control over, so he's not being naughty. He may also start staring at your plate because the sight of you eating will remind him that he will be fed soon, making him hungrier than usual. I always feed the dogs first, then they are happy and digesting their meal while I relax and eat mine.

f. Don't play tug-of-war as it allows the dog to pit his strength against you.

Tuggy is a great game to play, and many dogs really enjoy it. There are a few dogs out there that get hyper excitable with this game and it's not really for them. The rest love it and there is no sensible reason not to play. Dogs do growl when they are playing - especially this game. Your dog isn't growling at you and it will not teach him to be aggressive.

g. If you play tug of war, then the human must win the toy.

This is quite an amusing rule. Dogs don't really understand the concept of winning and if you do let go while playing, the dog may toss the toy around for a few seconds and then fetch it back to you, possibly rubbing it against your hand or leg to encourage you to play again. It's the game a dog enjoys, the interaction – not winning as this means the game is effectively over.

h. Keep the dog off the furniture.

There is no earthly reason why a dog cannot go on the sofa, except that you may want to sit there, and he is possibly big and muddy. This is a personal choice so don't feel guilty about cuddling up to your dog on the sofa. There is a small scattering of dogs that become selfish over the sofa and can get grumpy (see 9.14). No different to the dog that growls when it has a butcher's bone (see 9.15 – 9.18). We would obviously say 'no' to bones for that dog and never give them. Equally we should not let the grumpy dog guard the sofa from us – so those dogs shouldn't be allowed up. I stress it is only a <u>*small number*</u> *of dogs that do this – you hear about them because they make entertaining TV and internet articles. Just remember though, a dog doesn't know he's filthy so make your choice wisely. Many people put a dog blanket on the sofa and the dog is allowed up only when that is present – they learn this very quickly.*

i. Don't allow the dog upstairs.

Why? Again, this comes down to personal choice so don't feel guilty about having the dog in the bedroom – or the bed! Your relationship with your dog is unique to you. And if it causes no problems then there is no reason why not; vacuuming the bed is optional (see 9.13).

j. Confine the dog so he does not have free access into the living room.

This is about separating the dog from the family group so he's not part of the household. The aim is to make the dog more biddable and remove confidence by making him feel insecure and an 'outsider'. It kind of takes away the point of having a dog really. They like to be with us – they are social animals that love company. It is important not to allow young puppies the run of the house until house trained, or you may come across deposits that are several days old secreted under beds and behind laundry baskets! That's just common sense. You have to keep your eye on a puppy.

k. Don't allow a dog to lie in doorways as he is controlling the house.

You have to ask the question why a dog would want to lie in a doorway. These places tend to be cooler, so for the dog that feels the central heating it might be more comfortable. Some breeds herd and some are just plain nosey. As part of the herding instinct comes an innate awareness of where your group is. A doorway is a good place to mentally 'herd' the flock. The nosey dog (of which there are too many to mention) might find the doorway a useful place to be just in case, ensuring he never misses anything that might be beneficial. The opportunist nature is never far away in even the most devoted of dogs.

l. Take ownership of the dog's bed by sitting in it.

Possibly the funniest rule – and what's even more amusing is that people actually do it. And what is going through the dog's head at that time, I wonder? 'OK, you there. I'll take the sofa!' It would appear from my enquiries that many dogs try and get in with their owner or sit back head tilted looking perplexed. It would seem that they just don't get it.

m. Remove the dog's food while he is eating, to ensure you can.

It has to be said this is the quickest way to teach a dog to guard its food (see 9.15 – 9.17). Many dogs will accept food removal without a problem, but some will tense up, start growling and defend the food. And you have just achieved what you were trying to avoid. Better to add food to the bowl or just swirl you hand around in it for a second – handling the food but not threatening to remove it. Once the dog is relaxed with this you could take the bowl away and add more food – teaching the same thing in a less confrontational manner.

These rules were designed many years ago to create a dog who 'knows his place', but there seems little point in owning a dog if this is how you have to live with it and having a gerbil in a wheel might be a better option.

1.5 How Dogs Learn

Instead of thinking in terms of dominating our much-loved beastie in all areas of his life we need to focus on what matters. Concentrating directly on the problem and the situations where it occurs. What emotions drive this behaviour? What does he get from it? Has it simply become a habit? – as in, this is what *I* do in *this* situation.

Once we have understood this, our next challenge is changing the behaviour by doing any number of things like approaching the situation differently, responding in another way, avoiding any specific circumstances where we can, to directly teaching an alternative - for which we should really understand how he learns.

Interestingly dogs learn in the same way we do. They make connections between events and if an event has a good outcome then the behaviour accompanying said event is likely to be repeated. The opposite is true for a bad outcome. The behaviour that leads to a bad outcome may be tried a few more times just to be sure and then typically stop.

For instance, a dog will quickly work out whether you are leaving the house simply by the clothes you are wearing, the plucking of the house keys from their hook and the footwear selected. If an event has a good outcome (the donning of dog walking shoes is an example) he may run about the house squealing in anticipation and the subsequent walk would be deemed a success for the dog. So, the dog learns to run around the house squealing on the trigger of dog walking shoes being put on. If the outcome is not so good (perhaps a work jacket) then an entirely different emotion may be felt and relayed. This could be termed a failure for the dog – as he hasn't achieved anything of value for himself and faces losing his owner for a few hours. So, the dog learns to slink off to his bed and sulk. In dog training jargon these two are often termed positive and negative reinforcements. A bit of a mouthful.

Many years ago, I had a proper Heinz 57 called Mutley who accompanied me when I was lecturing. He knew when it was lecture day because I would have a box file placed by the front door (so I would fall over it on my way out of the house - I'm a scatterbrain). The file contained all my notes and slides and was crucial to the smooth running of the day. Mutley would always be sitting next to it in anticipation of an imminent outing, and the biscuits the college staff always provided, and my other dogs would be in their spots with a 'didn't want to go anyway' look. He'd learnt he was off out – they'd learnt they were stuck in.

Learning how to manage these daily successes and failures is in fact dog training and underpins all our day-to-day interactions. From house training through to managing serious behaviour problems.

1.6 Success

Success breeds confidence. The emotions felt can be anything from mild amusement to chest thumping euphoria although a dog's idea of success may not be the same as ours.

A dog successfully chasing off the postman each morning could well be in a state of jubilation. Raiding the bin can be successful sometimes and so can stealing from the kitchen surfaces – always worth a go just in case the dog gets lucky. Pulling on the lead is successful – but only if you pull hard enough. This success gets the dog to the lamppost quicker and to the park in record time.

If a venture is successful to the dog, he will repeat it.

When training our dogs, we are always attempting to make the behaviour we like successful to the dog and the stuff we don't like, unsuccessful. Sometimes we are trying to make the behaviour we like *even more fruitful* than what the dog likes to do. Coming when called is a good example of this (see 10.8). Running around is fun, so we have to make coming back *even more* fun.

1.7 Managing Success

Ensure the activities you like really work for your dog. The emotional connection the dog makes guarantees he understands what we prefer and what will earn him something great. Signals of success can include saying 'clever boy (or girl)' in a happy manner, praising through stroking and cuddles, rustling a treat packet, or making a specific sound, like a click.

A clicker is a small, hand-held device that clicks when pressed. The sound is the same each time the clicker is used and tells an animal when it has done something right (click = tick). The dog learns its significance by receiving a tasty food treat immediately after hearing the click. Often within three or four clicks and treats, the dog begins to look for the scoff on hearing the click. The click makes them feel successful, instantly. It then can be used as a marker – pinpointing something they have done as very good. Dogs learn quickly with a clicker, as they know straight away what they have done to get their treat. Once they get into the clicker 'game', they do things to try and make you click. They stop watching your hand with the treats and start focusing on the clicker hand. Offering you sits, downs, rollovers and paws, they try their very hardest to make you click.

Their trying harder is an emotional element we can harness to teach them something new. Holding back on treats creates feelings of mild frustration in most dogs – but only when they know the treats are available. This frustration drives them to keep trying and trying, and if that fails – to try something else. For example, if you stand in front of a dog holding a food treat, it will show interest. Many dogs will sit, in the hope that this will be enough. When the treat is not forthcoming, they might stand up and sit down again. This could be repeated several times until the dog eventually gives up on the sit and tries something else – maybe lifting a paw. This can then be marked with a click, and a treat given. This can be look at in more depth in Chapter 10 with some interesting ways to teach your dogs the basics.

The clicker can be replaced by the words 'good dog' or similar, however consistency in how it is said is paramount.

1.8 Motivating your Dog

Any reward or treat on offer must be intensely gratifying to the dog. Some are motivated by the prospect of getting food, others by physical contact or the opportunity to hold or play with a particular toy. Many years ago, when my training school was in a converted vegetable patch in my back garden, I helped train a Lurcher type dog called Nemo. His one love in life was bread. You could offer him best steak, chicken or top-quality dog treats, and he'd turn his nose up in favour of stodgy white bread. But whichever prize is used with the success signal (clicker or 'good dog'), go on motivating your dog to learn, and learn the things that work for you. Keep the sweeties coming!

1.9 Failure

This is awful. Really failing at something can make you feel sad, depressed, insecure and like you never, ever want to do it again. The depth of feeling associated with failure is often related to how much you wanted to succeed. But for our dogs we can help them to fail at the behaviour we don't like *and* compensate it with success for the stuff we do like.

1.10 Managing Failure

A success signal for your good behaviour should be balanced by equally clear-cut signals to show your dog he has failed to behave well and has done something you don't like. When a confidant dog realises, he's not going to get the treat he's hoping for, his mild frustration should spur him on to try other ways of getting what he wants. However, if you punish him physically, his behaviour may become unpredictable. Your dog will learn better when he doesn't feel threatened and has 'options' regarding what to do next. This helps him to control his feelings and make an educated choice.

Many people signal bad behaviour using a firm 'No!' This should be said in a displeased tone, as initially it is all about the tone of voice. I could say to a dog 'You're a nasty, smelly little beastie and I hate you' and he would stand and wag his tail at me as long as I said it in a nice voice. The tone is everything. Shouting does not really help in most cases as it can excite or frustrate many dogs, making their behaviour worse. If the dog doesn't stop using a simple 'no' and a displeased look, then a time-out would be a good idea for example, two minutes away from the family to calm down.

1.11 Time Outs

A time out is a calm and controlled method for dealing with poor behaviour and often a dog emerges from his two-minute segregation feeling quite chastened. For instance, say 'No!', he ignores you and continues what he's doing, so you immediately pop him in the porch, downstairs toilet (removing access to chemicals and paper products!), or outside. Then allow him back in as though nothing has happened by opening the door, walking away and ignoring for 30 seconds (see 1.13 – 1.15) so we don't reward the punishment through eye contact – this last bit is especially important - so you don't give mixed messages. Remember they learn through making connections between events and potential outcomes.

This technique strengthens the word 'No!' as suddenly there is a consequence rather like children and the naughty step. It is also very calm, passive even so as not to inflame situations, and avoids the need for harsher measures. It is very a very powerful tool.

Adapting this method for situations like barking at the front door are simple (see 3.14).

Harsher measures are sometimes required for very serious behaviour issues but should be avoided where possible by using time-outs or basic training (see Chapter 10).

These stronger measures could be something simple like a water spray, leading on to harsher deterrents such as a Pet Corrector™ or Bleep/spray collar. The key question you have to ask yourself before you embark on this route is 'have I done all the training and tried everything I can? For instance, if your dog is barking when he spies other dogs have you tried distracting him with treats or toys, have you trained 'leave it', (see 10.12) and implemented it correctly, have you tried adapting your time-out to be useful elsewhere (see 3.14). If the answer is yes and you have attempted these exhaustively, over a period of many months then maybe something stronger is justified.

1.12 Introducing a Dog to a Strong Failure Signal

The most important factor here is ensuring you do actually have a signal, a warning if you like, that your dog can follow. If you simply spray your dog with water when he's naughty the shock factor will quickly dissipate, and he will just get wet. The trick is to teach him a 'warning' that happens just before the punishment follows through, as it's important he knows what is going on. Just as we did with the word no followed by a time out. The word becomes the warning.

It is very straightforward to do but must be taught whilst the dog is calm and not whilst tackling the 'problem'. Put a nice goodie (pigs ear perhaps) on a chair or coffee table, not the floor. As soon as the dog makes a move for the goodie, spray him with the water and then show him the bottle and give a command like 'do you want this' spoken calmly. As he backs off ignore him completely – no eye contact. A few seconds later he may make a second attempt. This time show the bottle first and give your warning command 'do you want this?'. Now, you only spray if he does not stop. Either way ignore him completely for at least 30 seconds – no eye contact. At this point he may give up on the goodie and walk off or flirt with you outrageously. He may even run for the hills. At no point do you praise. Just act like nothing happened.

He may make further attempts on the goodie, to which you go through the same method, warning command, pause to see if he stops, follow through with spray only if he carries on. It's usually very quick for the dog to stop trying to steal the goodie simply on hearing the warning *And* seeing the bottle. But you must remember – no praise! Then you are ready to tackle your issues which should be done one at a time over a period of weeks / months so you do not overuse the spray as a dog will merely learn to ignore it. This method of using a failure signal allows a dog to make a choice – and we can only hope he chooses wisely.

If you chose to use a Pet Corrector™, then simply follow the advice above for the water spray. If you prefer a bleep/ spray collar, then use the bleep as your warning signal instead of your word or phrase. These products are widely available online.

1.13 Timing

It is crucial when doling out rewards or dishing out punishments that our timing is top notch. Rewarding too slow could incentivise the wrong behaviour - he learns all the wrong things. Punishing too late can also be disastrous, creating mistrust and anxiety. The golden rule is to reward or punish either during the act or within a second or two of it. You can't go far wrong if you heed this.

1.14 Mixed Messages

We are an inconsistent species. We have the ability to work out what our fellow humans want most of the time. Sadly, our dogs don't have this ability and we give them mixed messages all the time. Classic example is a dog jumping up.

Dog jumps up, is told to 'get off' or 'no'. Dog gets down and we say, 'good dog'.

We know that dogs learn through connecting events and the outcome of said event – good or bad – and then choose whether to repeat it or not. If the outcome is good its repeated…

So, by telling the dog it is good for getting off he in fact learns that jumping up equals good dog and will repeat it – because that's what we've taught him. Being careful with the use of our success signals stops the poor beastie getting confused and ensures we are actually teaching what we think we are.

1.15 The Thirty Second Rule

Think about adopting the thirty second rule. Indeed, if you take nothing else from this guide – do this bit. You'll be amazed at the difference it can make.

If you reprimand your dog in anyway then ignore it completely for thirty seconds. Now when I say ignore, I mean completely ignore. No eye contact (crucial), no speaking to or about the dog, (for instance no explaining to your other half what you are doing or asking what the dog's reaction is), no touching – obviously. This completely annihilates mixed messages – the ones that really matter at least. Initially it's good to count. Thirty seconds always feels like such a long time in this situation, and you must not short-change yourself. At the end of the thirty seconds act as though nothing has happened. For example, you are reading the paper, dog jumps into the middle of the paper, temporarily disrupting the pages. You say 'no' or 'get off' firmly and push him down. You carry on reading your paper without a glance right or left, or any further discussion. The dog is left in no doubt that you did not like what he just did.

Eye contact is a phenomenon. It can signal many things to other humans, and our pets. It can mean you are cross. It can be an acknowledgement of something. It can be an affirmation. It can also be flirtatious, a sign you are pleased with something or an expression of love. Best not to give eye contact after a reprimand as we don't know what our dog will make of it.

1.16 Quid Pro Quo

You do something for me before I do something for you. A great mantra for all dog owners and parents generally. Reduces the spoilt brat nature of the beastie and allows for a more balanced relationship. In essence asking your dog for a simple sit for dinner. Parents often do it with children – requiring them to clean their rooms before they get their sweets or pocket money. Otherwise, it's all take, take, take…

1.17 *Food Dispensing Toys*

Using toys that give out food treats is a marvellous way to feed dry food. It makes the meal last longer and actively stimulates the dog's scavenging nature – leaving it feeling fulfilled. They can be used to help with a variety of behaviour issues as you will see throughout this guide and you can use treats or dry dog food depending on the time of day. Some, like the Kong® for instance, allow you to put little scrapings of liver paste or peanut butter in to really impress the dog. There are numerous different designs in the marketplace and a selection of these rotated round can really inspire a dog.

1.18 *Sleep and Rest*

Many a behaviour case has been fast tracked by the subtlest change -increasing sleep and rest. Indiana, a three-year-old Weimaraner came to me a few years ago as he was being aggressive to his owners throughout the day. Interestingly he started the day off in reasonable spirits and became grumpier as the day progressed. In the session he wouldn't sit or lie down choosing rather to pace around restlessly. As we got talking, I noticed he had stopped moving, so I kept my eye on him. We were working through his average day and I looked up to see he was asleep, standing up. As I thought, Indiana's daily routine consisted of three walks, spread out, playtime in the garden and lots of inbetweeny activities including some training. Indiana's owner thought she was giving him everything – it was just too much!

Dogs need more than double the amount of sleep or rest than we do. I always work on the premise of eighteen hours out of twenty-four a dog should have its paws in the air. Not all at once for sure but broken up throughout the day in little doses. Overtired dogs are a problem. They can become manic, rushing around like hoodlums. They can be bitey and nippy, particularly when young. Chewing up things they wouldn't normally touch, jumping up at owners and generally being a nuisance. Worst case they become aggressive and grumpy. They are just like two-year-old children who've not had their afternoon nap. So, popping your dog off for a nap is not just a luxury – it's a necessity.

Sleep deprivation doesn't tend to cause problems on its own, (dogs who are grumpy at bedtime are an exception), it often makes problems markedly worse. The thief steals more often, the digger attempts Channel Tunnel II, the wrecker of toys broadens its areas of interest to encompass your toys (phone, remote control…) and bitey puppies become unbearable.

Many dogs don't settle easily if we are around. We move, they move. Teaching your dog, (from a puppy is easiest), to go to bed when tired often requires a crate or quiet place where it can be popped off for some uninterrupted sleep time (see 1.19). A radio playing calm music can help block out the noise you make moving around the house so the dog can properly switch off. A cover is useful to reduce the light and make the crate feel more like a den.

I teach my dogs to rest from young puppies by popping them in their crates for sleep breaks throughout the day. Usually within three to four weeks they've 'got it' and take themselves off to the sofa, crate or special place when tired. My dogs' daily routine is littered with rest breaks and I make a habit of not looking at them when I enter a room unless I want them for something, as it just keeps them on alert all the time.

1.19 Getting a Dog Used to its Crate or Doggy Den

Have the crate set up in the place you want it to stay. Put blankets or a crate mat inside and pop a covering over the top so only the door side is open. Put interesting toys inside to encourage the dog to go in and explore. Feed some meals in there only closing the door when the dog is going in happily. Allow the dog out once it has finished eating. Then get a tasty antler or similar and encourage the dog in, a small treat up to the nose and lure in if needed. Close the door calmly and quietly and let the dog eat its antler. Pop on the radio and walk out of the area or room. Go and do something else and ignore any complaints.

1.20 Formulate a Plan

Think about tackling your issues step by step. Do yourself a written list if needs be, in order of priority, starting with what annoys you the most first. That way you're not firing off on multiple tangents and having to make too many sudden changes to your life because in order to change your dog's behaviour, you will most certainly have to alter your own. Draw up the battle plan – broad outlines or minute detail as befits your situation, then stick to it. I've found that six to eight weeks minimum for each strategy normally starts to reap results – good or bad – so be prepared for the long haul. Like many people, dog's love routine, so be careful not to make too many changes too quickly, as this can be overwhelming for both dog and owner.

CHAPTER TWO

Indoor Toilet Trouble

2.1 Toilet Training or a Deeper Problem?

Messing in the house is unpleasant. Regularly cleaning carpets, washing curtains, and sponging down furniture can make dog ownership hard work. We first have to establish whether the problem is one of awareness – does the dog know where to toilet, or how to attract your attention to get access to it? – or if the issue is an emotional one because the dog is anxious, frightened or stressed.

Our dogs are naturally clean animals that prefer to toilet outside their home and preferably in the same or a similar place. If a dog has been house-trained and clean for a period of time and then begins to soil indoors, this may be an indication of illness. First stop – the vet, for a full check-up. Given a clean bill of health we can then look to tackle the problem. If he has never been fully 'clean', then we must assume he has never properly understood where the toilet is and needs to be re-trained from scratch.

2.2 Toilet Training a Dog from the Beginning

Take the dog into the garden regularly – every hour to begin with – and use gentle praise when a performance is given. Once his scent is established this then stimulates the dog to go in that area. Grass, gravel or concrete can then become a signal for going to the toilet together with this scent – a bit like when we see a sign for the loo, it can make us want to go. By giving a softly spoken word signal, such as 'wee wees', as soon as a dog crouches to perform, they can be quickly taught to toilet when asked which is great if you are on a schedule.

2.3 Dealing with Accidents

This method of toilet training is not only quick and safe, but also encourages the dog to toilet in one area in the garden or yard if that is what you need. If the dog goes to the toilet indoors and it is not immediately noticed, it should be cleaned away without any further reference. If he does it in front of you and you catch him red handed, say no firmly and put him in the garden while you clean up. Either way do not clean up in front of the dog.

2.4 Cleaning Up

It is important to use a cleaning product specifically designed for dog pees and poos. In their toilet is something called pheromones. These chemicals are difficult to get rid of as in a dogs' world they are needed for territory marking. Standard household cleaners do not do the job sufficiently to the dog's nose and a dog does like to toilet where its scent is, so not using the correct cleaner can encourage a dog to continually toilet in the same place, which is great in the garden, not so great up the fridge!

2.5 Signs a Dog Needs to Toilet

Watch a dog's body language for signs of circling, sniffing or looking agitated and you can often tell when it needs to toilet. Many dogs need to toilet after a sleep, a meal or play, and popping them into the garden at these times to relieve themselves helps with the training process. Go out with him and praise him for performing. There is no real need for wild praise or food rewards while toilet training, as the relief felt by going to the toilet is a reward in itself. Saying 'good dog' is often enough. Indeed, I would avoid using food treats as some dogs learn to lie to get the treat.

My Sproodle, Cricket, did this when I first got him as a youngster. He would go in the garden and squat, fixing me with a beady eye, and then run towards me wagging his tail in celebration for a food treat. The wet willy test outed him for the fraudster he was. His breeder had begun the task of house training and had used titbits as rewards, so Cricket being a wily creature, learned to fib!

He later expanded on his deception. I was out longer than intended, I can't remember why, and came home to a yellow lake in the kitchen. I ignored it and took the dogs into the garden and watched them. I was simply curious to know which one had been caught short. In an award-winning performance, they all crouched down and peed. So, I employed the wet willy test using a piece of tissue – Cricket was as dry as a bone…

Toilet training bells that you hang from your back door are a great help. Ring the bells every time you open the back door and very soon your dog will learn to jangle them to ask to go out.

2.6 Emotional Issues

Having decided that our dog knows where to toilet and how to ask, we have to look at his emotions and try and understand what could possibly be causing him to 'go' indoors. It may seem funny to link toileting problems with emotions but think about yourself for a minute. That trip to the dentist, the thirty minutes before an exam or a driving test – many of us go to the loo frequently at times of anxiety or stress. There is a natural reason for this; when we are stressed/

anxious our bodies are prepared to react immediately and so, in readiness, keep emptying out. This is all to do with the fight/flight system of self-preservation. When we go to the loo, certain chemicals are released in our brains that make us feel good. The brain reacts in the same way when we eat to satisfy our hunger, drink to satisfy our thirst, and during sex (supposedly!). It rewards us with a little burst of 'happy stuff' for answering our basic needs. When we are anxious or stressed these two things can trigger a little chain reaction all the way to the bladder or bowel – to make us go to the loo and feel better.

The same happens with our dogs, but unlike us they can't calm themselves with a slug of scotch or a nibble of chocolate and rational thought. Instead, a tense or nervous creature may choose to pee up the sofa or lay a cable in the hall in response to their anxiety (need to empty out in readiness to react) and to get their happy fix. When a dog is feeling very emotional about something, *one* of the things he may do is toilet.

Having something very scary happen to a dog while toileting can make him wary or frightened of that area. A dog with a bladder infection can be in great pain when it is peeing and may connect the garden with the pain and stop wanting to pee there. Constipation or diarrhoea can cause the same problem. A dog may be scared by a clap of thunder, or a bang from a car back-firing or firework while he's out in the garden and deem this a dangerous area to toilet. These animals need attention from the vet if they are ill and help to cope with their fear if they are frightened. Only then should you retrain them to mess where you want them to.

Excitement is also a factor. Ever had your shoes splashed by a wiggling puppy? It happens to me daily in puppy school. Most puppies grow out of this as they grow up and the bladder sphincter strengthens but it can take many months of mopping the floor and apologising to visitors. Greeting the puppy in the garden or on a lead on the driveway can reduce the mishaps. Telling a dog off for this is totally counterproductive as it is not doing anything on purpose. Keeping all greetings low key and calm can speed up the process. This is not something that generally persists into adulthood, but as adulthood varies from breed to breed, it can feel like a very long time.

Harvey, a working Cocker Spaniel, was a boot splasher as a pup but grew out of it. Owned by great friends of mine, he came regularly to class on a Saturday morning whereupon I was given a regular morning soaking. He had a particular knack of shooting the wee directly through his front legs, causing optimal elevation and I was left to conduct the group dripping from the knees down. I was tempted to put on Wellingtons and waterproofs and deploy an umbrella but instead settled for greeting him sideways!

2.7 Poos and Pees

Many dogs are confused and upset by being told off or smacked by their owners for going to the toilet indoors, and do not really understand why they are being punished, especially when the crime took place minutes or hours before. It may have been an accidental poo or pee, a result of being left alone too long, or feeling unwell, but it could be caused by anything that unsettles the animal, like a noise outside. Yet when the mess is discovered, the dog gets punished.

The next time the dog is left alone it feels concerned because it anticipates its 'parents' being cross when they arrive back. To relieve its anxiety the dog goes to the toilet – a natural reaction. Now the anxiety stakes have been raised even further, as the poo or pee lying there reminds the dog – having made the connection between mess and parental anger – that punishment is on its way. The dog looks guilty on the owner coming home, (in reality it is trying to mitigate the punishment). It is shown the toilet, punished and so the vicious circle begins.

Sparkey, a two-year-old Terrier, had always had erratic toilet habits. He had been housetrained using the outdated method of rubbing his nose in his mess 'until he blew bubbles'. He was then smacked and sent outside. Sparkey toileted indoors directly in front of his owners because he was afraid of them, and also in quiet, out-of-the-way places. The timing and forcefulness of the punishment varied, so Sparkey was never too sure whether what he did was right or wrong. There was little or no trust between Sparkey and his owners; they did not trust him to be clean – he did not trust them full stop!

This type of confusion, fear and anxiety can take many months to put right. Sparkey's owners gave him to a rescue centre stating he was a 'dirty dog', and I was put in touch with his new owners. We started from the beginning with house-training and confidence-building using a clicker (1.7), food dispensing toys (1.17) and clear, consistent communication (1.13 – 1.15). Toilet training was begun from scratch (2.2 – 2.5). After a few weeks of total consistency, Sparkey understood what was required of him and changed into a confident, happy dog.

It is crucial with these problems that you look directly at your dog on entering the soiled area with a calm face. Do not look around for any mess. That is the first part of the punishment process and we must eliminate it. Looking directly at the dog, say 'hello' normally and pop it into the garden. Clean the soiled area thoroughly while he is outside, using a specific cleaning product for dogs, and allow the dog back in as though nothing has happened. You must be sincere with this. Dogs read us like open books and know if we arc cross!

2.8 Coming in from the Garden to Toilet in the House

Some young dogs have such a brilliant time in the garden chasing about, that, like children engrossed with colouring in and filling their pants at the same time, they literally forget why they were out there. Coming indoors to pee or poo on the carpet does not make them popular! When house-training a rescue dog or puppy you should go out with them in the first few days but don't play or interact with them until after they have toileted. If a dog does come in from the garden and toilets and you catch them in the act, clap your hands or shout 'No!' and get them outside straight away. If you discover the indiscretion later, just clean it up thoroughly and go out with the dog the next time to ensure a toilet has been completed before you let them back in (2.2 – 2.5).

2.9 Toileting Overnight

A dog can be clean for many hours while you are out during the day, but toilet in the kitchen at night when you are sleeping. It could be that when you are out the dog switches off and is unconcerned. Knowing you are in the house but not directly with him could make the dog feel excluded from the family, and possibly leave him feeling anxious and upset. It may sound silly, but some dogs do not like the dark. Darkness can be linked to scary events such as fireworks or bright flashes of thunder (8.1 and 8.2). It is very common for a dog to be frightened or unsure of something only when it is on its own in a particular place – usually the time and place when it first experienced the fear.

Other reasons for feeling unsettled could be about where the dog is left. If left with free roam of the house during the day, being shut away at night could upset the dog. If a radio is left on when the dog is on its own during the day, then it could be the silence that is causing the bother. If the dog is young, or has just gone through the house-training process, don't leave newspaper or puppy pads down as this can stimulate the dog to toilet.

How we respond to the problem can often stop it completely, or at least stop it getting worse. Patrick, a three-year-old Sheltie, pooed and peed every night. Each evening before going to bed his owner would admonish the dog, telling him to 'be a good dog and don't go toilet on the floor'. Coupled with, standing over the dog and giving him a finger wag, this was quite scary. In the morning, lo and behold, Patrick had performed and was dragged to the stinking pile and told off. Patrick's owner was convinced the dog understood what he was being told in the evening, and even more certain the dog knew why he was punished every morning, because 'Patrick looks guilty' (2.6). Just stopping these encounters each morning and evening solved the problem in a few weeks.

2.10 Toileting When Left in the House Alone

Our dogs rely heavily on us. Our presence in the house makes them feel safe, secure and comfortable, and so it should. Sometimes they don't cope very well when we aren't there and can become frightened, anxious or panicky. These feelings can make a dog toilet somewhere in the house. How we react when we come home is important (2.6, 2.7 and 2.9), but so is helping the dog to cope better on its own, removing the need to mess. Deal with poos and pees when you get home in the same calm manner as first thing in the morning.

2.11 Dealing with Dogs Toileting When Left Alone

A dog can develop this habit just because you tell them off on your return (1.5, 1.13 – 1.15 and 2.3), but some dogs do it just because they don't like to be on their own. While it's not possible to be with your dog all the time, they are not designed to be alone and have to learn to deal with it. Help them to cope with isolation from the very first day they come to live with you. The kindest way is to leave them for a few minutes several times per day and increase this time over succeeding days and weeks. Make no fuss over leaving and keep all 'returns' light-hearted and low-key.

Dogs that have a toileting problem often need additional help to get over it. Dietary supplements that uplift their mood can greatly reduce their anxiety. They may need to be given for three to six months. Thundershirts™, Pet Remedy plug-ins, playing a radio, considering where a dog is left in the house, crate training – all should be considered to help the dog as much as possible. All these products are available online or in pet stores.

Cleaning up a mess thoroughly using cleaner that eliminates pet pees and poos can stop a dog being drawn back to the same spot time after time. Keeping to the same routine whenever you leave the house tells the dog what is happening – for example, give the dog a biscuit on his bed just before you leave. He may or may not eat it, but it is a clear signal to him nonetheless that there is no attention available from you. An even clearer way is to use Kong®, stuffed bones or antlers. Give him his antler just before you go, and then walk straight out. If using a Kong®, bone or antler, then pick this up when re-entering the house and put away for next time and keep this goodie specifically for when the dog is left. Leaving a radio on can relieve the worry of slight noises from outside or inside the house.

Bramley, an elderly Beagle, took to toileting when he was

left. He was used to being shut in the kitchen, and though we tried everything, the problem continued until the fridge broke down and had to be replaced. It was an old fridge, and quite noisy when turning itself on and off – and we realised he was scared of it! Many dogs can cope with these things when their 'parents' are around as they feel more secure. It is when they are on their own and the house is quiet that the 'ghosties' come.

Rescue dogs can have problems being left as they have been without a 'parent' for a while in the kennels. They come to rely heavily on their new 'parent', making it difficult for them to cope in their absence. As I've said above, going through a set routine like getting ready, picking up keys, popping the radio on, and producing an antler can help. Keeping any interaction with the dog to the barest minimum, go out and then come back in, a several minutes later. Repeating this regularly for a few days often does the job. Another little trick is to not pay the dog too much attention unless you specifically want it for something (1.18). Not giving eye contact on entering and leaving a room can help a dog to switch off and relax.

2.12 Leg-Cocking Dogs

Some males cock their legs high into the air to pee, and some just squat. The leg-lifters, particularly when young, may mark every lamppost, bush and gate on the daily walk – often pulling towards favourite spots to leave their 'I was here' mark. The mark consists of a few well-aimed spots of urine. This type of scent marking is different to normal peeing – a normal pee is a large quantity whereas a scent mark is a squirt. Many, including my current dogs, do a mixture of leg lifting and girlie squatting. They squat in the garden but lift their legs high out on walks.

Some females will squat down and raise one leg slightly

to try and squirt a few drops of urine.

Dogs leg-lift in the house for many reasons. The dog may be worried, looking for attention, feeling that the property is insecure, or perhaps there is a bitch in season around. Generally, it is dogs that have not been neutered that cock their legs in the house, but neutering them may not get rid of the problem entirely, as leg-cocking can quickly become a habit. If the scented areas are not cleaned thoroughly (2.4), a dog coming across a fading mark will feel compelled to top it up. A complete clean-up of all favourite peeing spots is unfortunately required, which may involve removing carpet and even changing curtains and furniture if they are beyond cleaning. Long curtains can be a particular attraction for the leg-lifter!

Stanley, a six-year-old Jack Russell Terrier, was an avid indoor leg-lifter. Having not gotten round to neutering him they did so on the vet's advice to stop the behaviour, but the habit persisted. His favourite spot was the full-length plush velvet curtains in the dining room. He didn't turn his nose up to a chair corner either – a detail his owners missed until (on my advice) they moved the furniture to check. Lo and behold there were little spots of yellow accumulating on the carpet. Cleaning the soiled areas thoroughly with the correct detergent (2.4) had Stanley firmly back on track.

A worried dog can be helped by giving it other things to think about, such as training it to sit, down, leave it and stay, and maybe teaching it a few tricks. This makes a dog feel successful because when he gets something right, he gets a reward. With success, confidence is increased, though this can only be achieved over a period of time. You can stop your dog from becoming even more anxious by not punishing him for his indiscretion unless he is caught red-handed. Ignoring a worried dog completely when he is showing signs he is concerned can help tremendously as acknowledging him in any way at that point can convince him there is something to be worried about. To be clear – ignoring means no eye contact, no speaking to or about the dog, no touching.

An attention-seeker will usually cock his leg right in front of you, looking directly at you. This chap wants you to notice him, and even if you tell him off, that is reward enough. You should look at how much attention he is given, how much sleep or rest he has had or not had (1.18) and how much 'fun' he has during the day. Some high-maintenance dogs need quite a lot to make them happy. Increase the sleep time if he hasn't had enough, games, exercise and contact through speech and touch using the 'quid pro quo' method (making your dog earn all rewards with simple sits and downs or similar, 1.16). If your time schedule is tight, look at using food-dispensing toys like Kongs® and swap all toys around so the dog does not have access to all of them all the time. This rotation of toys increases their value to the dog and holds their interest.

Females are in season for approximately three weeks and can drive all surrounding males crazy during that time. Here, the dog's leg-cocking comes from anxiety at not being able to do what comes naturally – the scent of a female in heat is strong and can last for many days. If a female is mistakenly brought to a training class when in season, none of the 'entire' males can concentrate and may start leg-cocking (up peoples' legs no less) and even fighting. Classes for the next few days will be disrupted even if the floor is cleaned. Castration or chemical castration (an implant that simulates castration) is the only real cure for persistent leg-lifting problems that are triggered by sex.

2.13 Diet Changes

Some dogs have sensitive tummies, and some are like garbage cans and can tolerate literally anything. Most dogs are fed a similar diet each day. This keeps the digestive system working well and 'output' normal. A sudden change to his diet can upset this, making poos loose and maybe causing him to be too slow to get outside. We do sometimes need to alter our dog's diet for a variety of reasons. Mix some new diet in with the old one – increasing the amount mixed in slightly at each meal. Take four to seven days over the change and your dog should experience no difficulties.

Treats should also be factored into this. If the stools are suddenly soft (Mr Whippies) and dinner is the same as usual, then look to see if any new treats or chews have been deployed.

There is no one diet for dogs, as they are all different. Some are better on canned food, some dry, some raw – you get the picture. When you find a food your dog both readily eats and tolerates well, then that is the perfect diet for him.

CHAPTER THREE

Being Noisy

3.1 Why Dogs Bark

Some dogs may bark a lot, others hardly at all. Perhaps their main motive is to let the family know someone is outside the house. Barking also indicates general excitement, like the dog that, when you pick up the lead, spins on the spot barking frantically in anticipation of going for a walk. A not-so-subtle form of communication, barking can indicate how a dog is feeling. While playing 'fetch' your dog may start to bark at you if you do not throw the ball quickly enough – displaying mild irritation. The barks sound different depending on why the dog is doing it, and most of us know what our dog is barking for, just from the sound of it.

3.2 Why Dogs Howl

Howling sounds soulful, and a dog with its head thrown back in full song can tweak the heartstrings of the strongest person. The main purpose of howling is to contact family members, and dogs rarely do this unless they are left without their owners. A howling dog can sound in serious distress, though this may not always be the case. Some dogs howl at certain pitches or sounds. My mother had a King Charles Spaniel that used to howl whenever she played Caruso on the stereo – very irritating for her, as she was a big opera fan, and she couldn't hear above the noise Gentil made. I know many dogs that howl at the sirens on emergency service vehicles, ice cream van jingles and also the theme tune to Coronation Street.

3.3 Emotional Issues

Dogs find barking and howling pleasurable for two different reasons. Firstly, these actions release chemicals in the brain, which makes a dog feel better – relieving boredom, anxiety, stress and frustration. For the anxious or stressed animal, that little burst of pleasure reduces the worry of being left – or the general worry of life. Dogs that are irritated and frustrated at being alone or ignored can relieve their annoyance through barking – often loudly and with gusto – with quiet gaps in between. Bored dogs do it because there is nothing else to do and it has simply become a habit.

The second reason is, if applied consistently enough, barking and howling works! The success of the activity spurs the dog on to do it again and again. Consider the animal that barks when the postman comes. The dog lays in wait for the postie, on full alert in anticipation of his appearance. As the postman approaches the house, the dog lets rip. The postman goes away – and the wayward pooch is convinced he has notched up another success. Although we know the postman was not coming in, the dog sincerely believes his actions stopped a potential intruder. He then applies the same actions to everyone who passes by, because it's good fun and makes him feel great (3.14). Dogs learn this sport all on their own without any help from us – and often barking at passers-by is the dog's main mental and physical stimulation for the day. For the dog who has been alone all day with nothing to do but bark, his owner coming home indicates that the barking finally worked. Job done!

3.4 *Being Noisy When Home Alone*

Most dogs switch off and sleep all day when their owners go out. Others find being left alone difficult to cope with. This may be because they are rarely left alone and have never really acclimatised to it, or at the other end of the spectrum they are left for far too long and it is unpleasant and lonely. As with all problems, the priority has to be understanding the emotional issues involved before tackling the habit. Managing the dog's emotions effectively can help him learn to deal with his situation appropriately. Simply getting another dog to keep him company is often not the answer. Without correctly addressing their emotional needs and breaking their antisocial habits, there is the strong possibility that both dogs will bark, making the problem much worse. The first dog barking or howling triggers the second to join in because it is a traditional group activity.

3.5 *Dealing with a Dog Barking When Home Alone*

Dealing with any problem that happens in your absence is tricky. Often, the owner has not even heard the dog bark and relies on neighbours reporting the problem, either directly or via the dog warden. There are cases where the dog only barks occasionally, but a dispute with neighbours about something completely different sparks a complaint about the dog. Enlisting help from the complaining neighbour goes a long way to resolving the problem, as you can then find out when the dog barks, how long for, and what type of barking – one bark repeated every few minutes, or a random burst of noise throughout the day. This information can indicate how the dog is feeling, and the reasons why he is being noisy. Once a behaviour programme is in place the neighbour can then report back as to its effect. If a helpful neighbour is not available, then leaving a webcam on while you are out can supply most of what you need to know – you may even be able to spy on your dog from work, but don't let the boss catch you!

A dog that barks at anything that happens outside will often bark randomly, and be more noticeable in the mornings, which are generally busier times in most neighbourhoods. This dog is doing his job, but perhaps a little too keenly. Toadie, a Jack Russell Terrier, was reported for his barking by angry neighbours. He barked at everything from deliveries to other neighbours, the postman and the milkman, and the poor neighbours got a mouthful every time they went into their garden or out of their front door. Some days he was relatively quiet, and others he was at it all day. His barking came in loud bursts lasting a few minutes. He also jumped up and sat in the front window in his excitement, leaving tell-tale dog snot on the glass and smashing several vases and ornaments. Toadie was not nervous, anxious or panicky – he was having fun, doing what some dogs do best – repelling potential boarders! There was no way of stopping his antics without blocking off the outside world, as this was the trigger.

Toadie was shut into the back of the house, away from the front window especially, and given a variety of toys, which were swapped round each day to give him 'new' things to play with. He was fed out of a variety of Kongs® including the Wobbler™ (1.17), and supplied with stuffed bones, delicious deer antlers (AKA stag bars) and other prime goodies. These were all hidden each morning around the kitchen and dining room for him to find. A radio was left on fairly loud (Classic FM for the refined mutt) to shut out noises that he would react to. Toadie's level of exercise was also addressed, and he was given an extra walk first thing in the morning, which included a ten minute off-lead session of ball-fetching to tire him out. This change in routine turned him from fervent house guarder to avid scavenger and he actually started to sleep during the day, helping him to be calmer generally (1.18). He still barked occasionally, but at a level acceptable to everyone and the neighbours were soon back on speaking terms.

A dog barking and howling periodically or continuously throughout the day is more likely to be suffering from anxiety or distress. The noise usually starts as the owner leaves, or within about half an hour. These guys are unlikely to take any interest in food toys, as their one aim is to get the parent back – but it is always worth a try. Consider what you do when you leave home and when you return, and you will be able to reduce the dog's emotional rollercoaster. A long, emotional farewell leaves him feeling more bereft, as he longs for the contact to continue. Equally, rapturous returns can make the dog anticipate this event even more.

Giving the dog a biscuit or a chew just before you leave can be an easy and consistent signal to the dog that you are now going (this does not stop them having a chew or a biscuit at other times, as they link events like you putting on coats and shoes when you are going out). Once the dog has his biscuit – leave the house. He may not eat it until you get back, but this is fine. When you get home say 'hello' to the dog but keep it low key and don't get into cuddles and big fusses for a few minutes. Ignoring a dog completely when you get home is unkind and the dog may feel punished by it, potentially making matters worse. He has waited for you all day, and the least you can give him is a smile and brief hello.

The essence of what we are doing here is to breeze in and out with the minimum of fuss and emotional disruption. Giving a natural calmer in his food and plugging in a relaxing diffuser can also help the dog's anxiety and enable him to chill, as can many other products such as calming collars and Thundershirts™ (a body wrap). Try different ones to see which works for your pooch – keep them going for a minimum of six weeks for each before you change or you don't give them the chance to work. This significantly speeds up a learning process that can take many months.

Sandy was a small Crossbreed that lived with a married couple who then got divorced. Mum took a job and was out for six hours per day. Sandy had never been left for long periods and found this hard to deal with and so started barking (a bark followed by silence, followed by a bark). He was also a little traumatised by the break-up – insecure and less confident generally. Sandy followed his mum around the house all the time, which he had previously not done. To help his confidence we started a trick-training campaign, where Sandy earned nice treats through successfully learning and performing tricks. Earning rewards through any type of training can help a dog to feel successful, thus increasing general confidence (1.5 – 1.7). He loved it, but most importantly his owner loved it and did loads of tricks and basic obedience with him. Using a natural calmer in his daily diet also helped reduced his fears (although she did have to try several), and his confidence returned in a few short weeks. His owner also kept her leaving and returning routine short and sweet, and Sandy was back to his old self in no time.

Rhythmic barking (a woof every minute or two) shows a dog is controlling his frustration or anxiety. The repeated woof gives the dog a small burst of pleasure, making him feel better for a short while, but he then needs his pleasure topped up! Using a mood up-lifter (as with Sandy above) can add to his sense of pleasure and take away the need to get it by barking.

You may solve a dog's emotional problem but still be left with an acquired barking habit. In such cases the use of tasty stuffed bones or deer antlers could be the answer as it is difficult to bark and chew at the same time. Chewing is also a way of relieving stress or frustration.

Looking at where the dog is left in the house can also be useful, as with Toadie. Many dogs feel happier in places where they spend a lot of time with their owners (or there is comfy seating), so take this into consideration also.

There are anti-barking collars available – some which vibrate or emit a high-pitched noise, and some that squirt out compressed air. I haven't had to recommend one in quite a few years so would suggest trying the above and allowing plenty of time for changes to take place (a few months) before investing your hard-earned money. I would say, though, that the use of electric shock collars will probably cause you many additional problems (often fear-related) and I cannot recommend them under any circumstances.

Poppy, a delicious Springer Spaniel, had mastered the art of maintaining a regular and periodic bark interspersed with the odd howling aria. During the evening and night, she had the run of the house and chose to sleep by her owner's bed. She followed him everywhere when he was around, even curling up on the bathmat when he was taking a soak. When he went to work, he locked her in the kitchen as many people do and so, feeling miserable, she entertained the neighbours with her painful renditions.

Poppy took to wearing a Thundershirt™ straightaway and she visibly relaxed when it was put on. Coupled with giving her the run of the house (no prizes for guessing where she slept), the howling and barking gradually reduced over a couple of months. The next-door neighbour was hugely relieved at this – she had never been annoyed by the noise as is usual with cases like this, she just felt huge pity for the poor dog.

3.6 Coping with a Howler

It really is a 'please come back' cry to the parent (although joining in with a neighbouring howler is rare but can happen). Soulful howling can make neighbours upset, out of concern for the dog. Ellie was a shaggy Crossbreed who was shut in the kitchen while her owner was at work. She was quiet in the morning but howled all afternoon. This was because her owner came home and spent every lunchtime with Ellie, taking her out for a short walk and playing with her. Ellie could cope with the mornings but being left twice was more than she could bear so she sang her heart out to get mum back – which of course worked as her owner had to come home sometime. Stopping the lunchtime visit home and leaving Ellie all day kept her emotionally stable and quiet.

3.7 Spinning, Barking, and Biting as You Leave the House

A dog that feels intensely annoyed at the prospect of being left can develop a temper tantrum. It is usually just when you are leaving that the dog erupts in a whirlwind of activity which can include barking, spinning, jumping around or up at you and, in some cases, giving you a nip, perhaps to try and hold you there physically. These guys tend not to bark all day or do anything else except for show their extreme displeasure at you going. Compensation is the key here. The dog doesn't want to lose the reward of having you around, so you need to make him feel better (or even happy) about your going. This is where special food rewards come into play. Let him play with a Kong® stuffed with tuna, ham, or chicken – or an interesting mix of all three (1.17). Marmite, peanut butter or cream cheese smeared around the inside can whet the appetite of the most pernickety creature. It is amazing how quickly a dog can alter the way it feels when offered something wonderful, and how speedily they can change their allegiance from us to the Kong®!

Get the Kong® ready while the dog hovers in the background. His anticipation will clearly show as he begins drooling. Put the Kong® in the dog's bed and it will be leapt on with great eagerness as you back towards the front door, sincerely believing (and almost hoping) that your dog will show at least some interest in your departure. And yes, you will get a quick glance, albeit a fleeting one as the dog nods a farewell, unwilling to leave its new prize for a second. Overlooked for a piece of red rubber!

If the dog seriously enjoys telling you off it may leave the Kong® to do so, knowing it can return safely to it in the basket. These guys need to be outwitted. Carry the Kong® to the door with you and then roll it across the floor away from you as the dog approaches. If it is stuffed with the correct amount of 'yumminess', one sniff and the dog will have it and be gone.

With a well-trained dog you can simply use your obedience training coupled with the 'goody' as the prize. The good old sit-stay in the hallway perhaps, rewarding the dog by throwing the treat (antler, bone, food toy) as you close the door. Another to try could be sit and wait, place the goody a couple of metres away (like dinner time), and then a simple 'OK' as you close the door. Problem behaviour is always easier to solve when the dog has good training to utilise (see Chapter Ten).

3.8 Barking at Strangers, Dogs and Other Animals

Shouting is some dogs' idea of a good time. Barking at everything that moves – cars, bikes, cats, horses and people – can be first-class entertainment. A dog is not necessarily aggressive when it is barking but can be hugely over-excited. And your reputation suffers simply because your dog makes so much noise on a walk. You can't even try walking him at one o'clock in the morning, in case he sees a fox or a cat. You become 'that person' with 'that dog!' Ignoring the dog's behaviour gets you nowhere because he is having a great time and couldn't give two hoots about how he is making you feel. Shouting and yanking him about on the lead only adds to his excitement. Take the sport out of this activity and make the dog think again about how he has fun.

An errant Border Terrier from a village near me had a huge reputation for such a small dog. Everyone knew Teddy. The receptionist at the local vets cringed when he walked in, knowing the waiting room would be in uproar. Neighbours crossed the road to avoid him in the street. The local horse-riding fraternity would trot off in the opposite direction to avoid possible injury from their horses being startled. It was a nightmare for Teddy's owner. Being a small place, everyone knew everyone else. Although Teddy meant no harm, he would scrabble and dance on his back legs, barking his head off at the mere sight of something moving.

A bleep/spray collar was used to modify his behaviour and take the fun out of it. As soon as Teddy began to react, he would hear the bleep (1.12 – 1.14). It was then his decision whether or not to continue and get a dose of the spray. Teddy chose wisely. His owner then began to reward him with nice titbits – corned beef was his favourite. This distracted his attention from the moving object and helped him to concentrate on his owner when she wanted him to.

Walking a dog on a head collar, like a Gentle Leader or similar, instead of a normal collar can also reduce a dog's excitement and have a calming effect (10.7). Leave it training (10.12) can work well on the dog that doesn't get too het up.

Some dogs take great exception to animals appearing on the television and enjoy chasing them off, sometimes knocking the TV over in their excitement. A very large

Mastiff, belonging to a friend of mine, had a bad habit of doing this. Not only did he damage the TV he also took to watching it whenever it was on – waiting for his next victim to make an appearance. Tiny's hulking frame blocked all evening viewing until a well-aimed water pistol, squirted at him from behind when he took up position, changed his mind (see 1.12 – 1.14).

Over the years, two of my dogs have watched TV. Strumpet, my Pug, particularly enjoys anything with animals, preferably horses, and loves a period drama (the only mode of transport back then). Indeed, any Dickensian style of programme can keep her rapt attention. Strumpet is also a great supporter of rugby, particularly enjoying the kicking game as the ball flies through the air. If she starts barking, I simply put my hand over her face so she can't see, and this calms her – easily done because she is always on my lap. I used to have a special needs Staffie, Pumpkin, who was brought up with small children before she came to live with me. My friend (her previous owner) had children's TV on much of the time, so CBeebies was the programme of choice. Pumpkin didn't become wildly excited at the TV, she simply became absorbed in it, to the consternation of the wild Springer, Parsnip, who couldn't understand what she was looking at and why she wouldn't play!

3.9 Barking for Attention

This is a particularly irritating and embarrassing habit – rather like a child that plays up in company and leaves you feeling incompetent as a parent. The attention-barker looks directly at you when he does it. His barks are loud and forceful – designed not to be ignored. This is one area where ignoring the barking does work – eventually. But you have to be prepared to go through the ear 'pain barrier' first. Ignoring the barking makes the dog try harder to gain attention, barking louder and louder and becoming more frustrated at not getting what he wants – even the most devoted owner can be forgiven for caving in. A dog like this needs to learn how to handle his frustration when he doesn't get what he wants immediately.

Clicker training is a wonderful way of teaching a dog to cope with frustration. The dog knows food is on offer but has to do something right before getting the click. The click tells him what he has done is right, and then he gets the treat (1.7). Food-dispensing toys can have the same effect (1.17). But teaching a dog to manage its emotions better is only half the battle. The other half is to make sure his bad behaviour doesn't work for him. If going through weeks (sometimes months) of ignoring a dog that is barking right in your face is not for you, then consider using one of the suggestions in 1.12 or better still, simple calm time-outs (1.11 – 1.15).

Mollie, an elderly Labrador, was a prolific barker. She barked at many things, but if her owners were not paying her copious attention, she especially barked at them, seemingly right in their faces. Rather like a cantankerous old lady with a summoning bell! 'Give me attention and give it now' was ringing out loud and clear from Mollie and, embarrassingly, she did this in front of visitors and in the street if either of her owners dared to stop and chat to neighbours. Telephone calls were made from alternative rooms or the garden and visitors were discouraged.

Mollie also had arthritis and as it was the winter months when her barking worsened, I encouraged them to visit the vets for a check-up. The vet prescribed anti-inflammatories and strict rest, with exercise to be built up slowly from five minutes twice per day by five minutes each week. This restricted me a little when looking at relieving some of the attention-seeking, so we settled on time-outs as a passive and not too active way forward. Mollie was calmly removed from the room the instant she started her irritating behaviour and allowed back in two minutes later. There was much innings and outings for several weeks but finally Mollie started to get the message. Telephone ringtones were also altered regularly to reduce the chance of Mollie learning new triggers.

Mollie still barks, but not for long and the incidents have reduced. It takes a long time to change an older dog's behaviour, and much persistence on the part of the owner. The time-outs have helped in reducing the reward Mollie felt (by receiving attention) and ongoing management of the arthritis played its part by helping Mollie to feel generally better.

3.10 Barking When You are on the Telephone

We automatically walk quickly to the telephone when we hear it ringing. To the dog this means a sudden burst of household activity when they hear the ring, and he joins in the race to answer it, sometimes barking all the way. To avoid a dog doing this, try getting up slowly and walking calmly to the phone. Changing the phone to a completely different ring and then answering it without rushing can also help. As with all behaviour that seems rewarding, the persistent offender may require this fun element to be removed in order to stop (1.11 – 1.15).

The attention-seeker that is affronted by you caring more about the piece of plastic in your hand than them, may bark directly at you throughout your conversation. A water-squirter kept by the telephone can be directed at the dog and a warning command spoken, followed by a quick burst sprayed out – right in the chops! – if the warning is not heeded. By teaching the dog about the water sprayer beforehand (1.12 – 1.15), you ensure this approach is much more effective in the long term and avoid a sopping wet dog. If you prefer a less offensive approach, then a nice chew can be kept in a drawer near the phone and given to the dog as compensation for ignoring him for a few minutes. Remove what is left and put it back in the drawer for the next call. This may not be suitable if your telephone rings all day – the dog at some point will get full! A toy kept especially for this can be a great alternative, but beware the loud squeaker, as you may not be able to hear what your caller is saying.

Tilly, a Standard Poodle, craved her owner's attention in many situations. The most problematic was her barking whenever 'Mum' spoke to visitors or on the telephone. Tilly sometimes became so annoyed with the telephone that she started biting at it. Her owner used a combination of treats and a water pistol, keeping both in her apron pocket. Having taught Tilly what the 'gun' was all about (1.12 – 1.15) she got a friend to call a few times and simply showed the pistol to Tilly, using the phrase 'do you want this?', which soon stopped the noise. But Tilly was still very frustrated and paced up and down, biting chunks out of the cheese plant to vent her spleen and get attention. Her owner then started throwing pieces of food for Tilly to chase and capture as soon as she picked the telephone up. This dual approach told Tilly clearly that barking was no longer fun, the reward was in finding the food. Using a game of fetch with a ball, as well as throwing treats, stopped Tilly getting fat!

3.11 Barking in the Garden

Keeping a dog outside during the day might be nice for them and you, but may be a burden on the neighbours. The need for toys and stimulating distractions is as important for a dog kept outside as for one inside – sometimes more so. Neighbourhood noises are louder, and the dog may react to things out there that he would ignore inside. Most complaints from neighbours about barking, concern dogs left outside all day.

Pasha, a Samoyed, was shut out all day because he would poo and pee if left in the kitchen when his owners were at work. They left for work at six o'clock in the morning and Pasha began barking soon after. It was but a few days before neighbours were telephoning complaints through to the dog warden. Bringing Pasha back into the house and dealing with the toileting issues resolved the dispute (2.11). Shutting a dog outside because it has a problem inside is side-stepping the issue and not resolving it.

Going out into the garden is exciting. There may be cats, birds and squirrels to swiftly despatch by barking at them, or just the opportunity to run around and let off a little steam. Many dogs like to shoot out of the back door barking excitedly, doing a lap of honour to tell all the neighbours 'I'm here'. This may be fine during the day, but can become a problem in the evening, particularly in the summer when folk have their windows open and have settled down to relax for the night. A simple solution could be to put the dog on a lead for his 'last pee' and take him up the street (with a poo bag for cleaning up), or out into the garden, letting him off the lead after a couple of minutes of calm. Teaching him to sit and stay at the back door before you open it may take some of the wind out of his sails. A local dog training school can help with this but following the steps in Chapter Ten might do the trick. If these techniques don't provide the required results, consider removing the fun out of the behaviour using one of the suggestions in 1.12 – 1.15.

Children next-door may wind a dog up by banging on the fence or hanging over it. This is potentially dangerous for the children as all dogs have their boiling point, however placid they are. Some friends of mine have a beautiful Mastiff. He was being teased by children next-door and was barking a lot in the garden. Having gone around and explained to the parents the dangers of what their children were doing, to no avail, my friends asked me for help. I went around with a bleep/spray collar to help out (1.12 – 1.15) and was amazed to see that the father next-door was joining in with the children. He thought it was funny to wind up a full-grown Bull Mastiff. What a nutter! My friends moved to a new house before their dog lost his rag.

A reverse time-out can also be hugely useful for this problem. Instead of the dog being put out, he's brought in. This will only work though, if he comes in easily from the garden or is easy to catch. A wily dog may change his barking habit into a chase-me game without you even realising it.

3.12 Barking During the Night

Whether it is dashing through the dog flap to chase off a fox, barking in the kitchen because it is anxious, or reacting to a noise outside, barking during the night is not acceptable for owners or neighbours. Sleep is important to us; we cannot catch up on sleep during the day like a dog can.

One lady brought her very angry Crossbreed to me because it was barking in the night. She didn't seem to mind that it tried to kill every person it came across, me included. In the behaviour session the dog sauntered calmly around my coffee table and wagged its tail as it approached my knees, giving off lovely cuddly signals – and then changed into a snarling monster ready to rip my face off if I made one false move. It was wearing a muzzle, but somehow, I was not reassured. The owner laughed jauntily at this, and said, 'Oh she doesn't like people very much, but then neither do I,' and, patting the dog on the head, she took hold of its collar and sat it back beside her. Convinced that the dog understood every word she said, she began relaying the information I gave her to the dog, albeit in simple child-like terms, while the dog sat cutely with its head going from side to side as it absorbed the information. I was tempted to give the dog a written test at the end to ensure it had fully understood what was going on.

In fact, the problem was easy to resolve as the dog barked whenever the next-door neighbour went in or out, and he left for work at some ungodly hour. Moving the dog into the bedroom and away from the front of the house was a simple, and well received, suggestion. I could have gone into lengthy reasons why the dog couldn't understand her, and made possible suggestions as to why she was aggressive, but what was the point? The owner was happy; she had read all the books on dogs and decided they simply did not apply to hers. I escaped another behaviour session intact, having counted my fingers and toes, but I filed her case notes not under 'B' for barking, but 'BM' for barking mad!

Simply moving the dog from an area where it is readily disturbed can stop sleepless nights. Having a dog sleeping either on your bed or in a basket in the bedroom or on the landing is your personal choice. It may be that the dog prefers the living room to the kitchen and giving it the freedom to choose may do the trick. I have never shut a dog in the kitchen overnight as I like mine to have the run of the house. I remember as a child our Boston Terrier, Puffin, being religiously locked into the kitchen at night. He would work away at the 1970s sliding door until free and then scoot up the stairs and onto my bed. Thirteen years, this went on for, and yet every night he was shut in the kitchen once more – futile! If giving free rein at night keeps the dog settled and happy (and you can cope with the dog hair) there is absolutely no reason not to do it. I have done so all my life.

Some dogs do like a crate. Indeed, they feel safe, happy and relaxed in a crate. These feelings of safety can help a dog to relax, so this method for bedtime might suit your dog. Always remember that all dogs are different, and what works for one doesn't work for another, so an open mind is always needed.

3.13 Barking in the Car

Sorry to mess you about – I felt it important that you could access help for this issue under the 'barking' section, but this subject is comprehensively covered in Chapter 6 – Travelling Issues.

3.14 Rushing to the Front Door Barking

Being a very territorial animal, dogs are great at guarding our houses from all and sundry. But they can be just a little too hair-trigger – rushing off at any noise or perceived noise coming from the front or back of the house. Most of us appreciate this, it's good to know if there is someone about, but not if done excessively like 'the boy who cried wolf'.

We won't stop a dog barking as it's a natural behaviour, but it would be good to temper it down a notch. This can be easily achieved by saying 'enough'. Initially a dog will keep barking so we need to follow it up. Time-outs work really well for this (1.10 and 1.11).

Give the signal 'enough' once the dog starts barking at the door. Only if he continues pop him in the time-out place. After the two minutes allow him out, don't forget your 30 second ignoring (1.14 and 1.15) as we mustn't give mixed messages. Repeat until the dog stops on just hearing the word 'enough'. Do not be tempted now to tell him he is a good boy, or you will end up encouraging more barking…

My old Pug, Strumpet, is a clever old stick. If she wants the other dogs out of her way she will rush in the direction of the front door and bark a couple of times. Just the other night, Pancake the Cockapoo, was lying by my feet gnawing on a buffalo horn directly in Strumpet's way. Strumpet, being old, can no longer jump on the sofa and requires me to lift her –

but she couldn't get to me. So, she did a 2-metre dash in the direction of the door, squealing like a strangled parrot (like Pugs do). Pancake rose to the occasion and sprinted off like a missile and Strumpet was able to get to where she wanted to be. Sometimes barking can be very useful to a dog.

3.15 The Myth About Training a Dog to Bark

There is a method of stopping barking that's been doing the rounds for years namely teaching a dog to bark on cue and then never giving the command. It came about at the same time as clicker training. This simply does not work because dogs bark instinctively. It is part of their natural make up. It is not something we teach them, therefore not something that can be eradicated completely.

CHAPTER FOUR

Being Destructive

4.1 Destructive Behaviour

Dog's chew, dig, and scrabble with their feet. They can create devastation in a few short minutes with their scratching and gnawing. You may object to your dog eating its way through your prized possessions, digging through walls (I once met a Staffie that had dug a Hobbit hole from the hall through to the kitchen, see 4.6) and destroying your much-loved home. After all, you expect a certain amount of respect for the house you all share. Dogs do not destroy your things to get at you. This is the sort of action a human being might take out of spite or revenge and is not part of a dog's make-up as it involves pre-meditation and often a bit of preparation.

4.2 Emotional Issues

As with toileting (Chapter 2) and barking (Chapter 3), dogs can become destructive for a variety of reasons. Youngsters who, like babies, explore new objects with their mouths, can chew or even eat household items simply because they are there. As boredom creates feelings of frustration a bored dog might eye up a magazine or cushion and relieve its monotony by shaking or ripping it up – great fun! An anxious dog can gnaw on wooden doorframes, furniture, or anything it can get its jaws around. Chomping and grinding on something can alleviate anxiety, much as humans chew gum. Puppies have a tendency to nibble at houseplants, just because they are there! It is normal for a dog to chew. It is what and where they chew that can be the problem.

A dog scratching at the back door may simply indicate it needs a pee, whereas a dog scratching at the kitchen door when he's been locked in could be signalling anxiety. Digging in the house on carpet, lino, a sofa or mattress can indicate a dog in panic, but again could be a great stress reliever, or an activity to break up the monotony of the day. If your dog is seriously afraid of staying where he is, trying to dig his way out is a distraction and a relief. If it makes him feel much better, he'll try it again and again.

4.3 Boredom

This is the most common reason for dogs chewing. We forget that, even when they grow out of puppyhood, they still need toys, bones and stimulating objects to give them something to do. In the absence of anything else, a nice pair of shoes can make for a pleasant diversion. You may think a toy box stuffed with interesting bits and pieces will keep the dog busy, but if it's always left lying around it may soon lose its appeal. Like us, they can get bored with what's familiar, and will be more entertained if you present them with a toy they haven't seen for a while. Keep up their interest by rotating their toys – and by joining in occasionally with a game like fetch or tuggy (10.14). I used to own a large hairy Crossbreed called Bigun. He discovered a ball in the garden that he had previously buried and spent the next two hours throwing it up in the air and chasing it. Our dogs have lots of balls, but this one had extra appeal because he had not seen it for a while. If you are out at work during the day just be aware that your dog may need a bit more of your attention in the evening.

Things to do could be feeding through training, out

of food-dispensing toys or by scattering (dry food only). Ensure your dog is properly exercised for his age group and vary the walks so they remain interesting. Play games, rotate toys, possibly groom your dog if he enjoys it. Allow your dog to be with you while you are at home – sometimes that is enough.

4.4 The Irritated Dog

A dog, like a child, can get cross when it sees things going on it wants to join in with, but can't. A closed door or window with an animal or person on the other side can wind the dog up into a frustrated frenzy. They may take their irritation out on anything that moves (owner or other household pet walking by) or, if all else fails, a cushion. Net curtains and blinds are also a popular target, as they interfere with the view. Give them other things to focus on by keeping them well exercised and mentally occupied using food toys or great chews like antlers and buffalo horns. If they get cross in a particular place, such as in the living room with people walking past the front of the house, block their route to it with furniture, or just keep the room door closed.

Duke, a rather large and hairy German Shepherd, would dig holes in his owners' bed when they were out at work. He was not a nervous or panicky dog – on the contrary, he was very confident and playful. Seeing people and other dogs walking past the house always made him excited, and when his owners were home and he was allowed in the living room, he would grab cushions and jump onto the sofa and scrabble around. But when his owners were out and the living room was closed to him, he went straight to the bedroom – and with no one to stop him he scrabbled right through the mattress. Like many German Shepherds, he could open doors with handles and knobs. The answer was to turn all the door handles upside down and to keep him out of rooms with windows overlooking the road when his owners were out. Easy, practical solutions are always the best.

4.5 Eating the Mail

The post or newspaper coming through the letterbox is a prime target for the eager mutt. As post and papers don't always arrive at the same time each day, you can't always be around when they do. A cage attached to the letterbox will catch the post so the dog can't get to it. It doesn't take the fun out of trying, though. A post-box on the outside of the house can reduce or completely stop the dog's efforts, as he may not even realise the postman has been. You must get a secure one though that someone cannot remove post from by putting their hand in, or you may be a victim of fraud. A porch is wonderful if you can afford it. Using methods like a time out (1.11) or the suggestions in 1.12 – 1.15 can help when you are present, and possibly denying your dog access to the front door when you are not at home could be a good way forward.

4.6 Destructive When Left Alone

When our dog is alone in the house, we don't know what he is getting up to – or why. If he starts destroying things, we often have to use educated guesswork to get to the root of the problem. A serious mess can tell us that he was really getting stuck in but will not reveal the emotion behind it. For example, a dog that ate its way through a sofa could be in great distress and trying to dig a hole to hide, or it might have picked at a corner of a cushion, discovered the white fluffy bits inside, and had a great time unstuffing the rest. The dog's personality may provide more clues. A nervous type is perhaps more likely to destroy through anxiety than a confident, relaxed individual. A self-assured individual is more inclined to munch at things, because it is under-stimulated.

Where the damage occurs and what has been ruined can tell us more about the animal's emotional state. If a door is scratched from the inside, or the wallpaper and wooden frame by the side of the door are damaged, then the likelihood is the dog is unhappy and trying to get out. Likewise chewing marks on the carpet or rug by a closed door could indicate the dog was trying to escape.

Elsa, a three-year-old Staffordshire Bull Terrier, was steadily digging and eating her way through the wall that divided the hall from the kitchen. In fact, she had almost completely finished her Hobbit-hole enterprise and daylight could clearly be seen. She was shut in the hallway when her owner went out, and at no other time. The main living area where everyone congregated was the kitchen. The wall was about six inches thick, and Elsa was a very determined young lady. When she ate through the telephone cable and the phone was cut off her owner decided enough was enough.

Elsa was anxious about being left, but only because she did not feel happy in the hall. Punishing her when her owner got home from work each day created more of an anxiety problem, as the digging had occurred minutes or hours earlier (1.13, 2.7 and 2.11). Elsa became anxious at the thought of her owner arriving home. As she had been pulled over to the mess she'd made, shown it and smacked, the sight of this scared her as well. Relieving her anxiety by stopping the punishment on return and not acknowledging the mess, giving her a natural calmer, a mood-elevating dietary supplement to help relax her a little, and allowing her to stay in the kitchen where all her toys were, together with a nice comfy chair to lie in, made all the difference.

It's a very similar problem to toileting indoors and barking at night. Trying different places for the dog to stay in when left alone or giving the run of the house or confining to a crate often is the answer to a happier dog that doesn't dig or chew when left. I meet people who tell me they would never use a crate, never let their dog in the living room etc. And they all have their reasons, such as thinking it's cruel to crate a dog and living rooms are for humans only. All our dogs are individuals, each with their own needs, likes and dislikes. What works for one will drive another potty. There is no one-size-fits-all solution. You have to be open minded and work through issues systematically to help the dog to behave well.

Max was a year-old Labrador when he was first left alone for several hours. He had a magnificent time whizzing in and out of the dog door to the garden. Having dug several large craters, he turned his attention to the garden furniture, chewing large chunks out of the wooden table. The flowerbed was not overlooked, and a few blooms were plucked, and others dug up completely. While he was doing this it rained, so his digging got him covered in mud. He went back into the kitchen, padded his muddy paws around a bit, tore a hole in the tea towel, and nicked the oven gloves, taking them off to his bed for a more comfortable nibble. His owners were horrified when they got home to find the wreckage and a very muddy but happy pooch wagging his tail at them – pleased with his day. Max was a very confident, almost independent dog. He enjoyed entertaining himself (evidently) and didn't follow his owners around, except out of curiosity to see if there was anything going for him. The level of damage was such that they sought professional advice straight away.

Max had got bored making him feel frustrated and found entertainment in his own way. The rubber bone that had been left for him to play with was untouched. He had found far more interesting things to do than lie in his bed and chew rubber.

The answer was to give him his morning meal in food-dispensing toys, which he had to go looking for once his owners had left for work. They also bought him a variety of toys and rotated them, so he had something different to play with each day. A professional dog-walker was hired to take him out for a long walk just before lunch. She settled him down again for the afternoon with an antler kept especially for this time and his owners made sure one of them was home at a reasonable time. The dog door was locked – too much temptation! All this successfully distracted Max from his destructive behaviour.

Being very afraid can also cause a dog to be destructive. A dog can literally be afraid of anything – as can we. In the case of Emma, an elderly German Shepherd, it was fireworks, but it took us many weeks of treating her for anxiety before we realised it. After nine years of never touching anything and always being shut in the kitchen when left, Emma suddenly became destructive, scratching at the kitchen door and frame, desperate to get out. She had not responded at all to our behaviour programme – she had not improved, nor had she got worse (when a pet's behaviour worsens, do the opposite of what you have been doing and that usually sorts it). I was about to give up, when a chance comment about a firework party in the garden helped me realise what was wrong. Her owners had shut her in the kitchen while they let fireworks off. Emma felt that the kitchen was dangerous (8.1 and 8.2), but only when she was in there alone and the door was shut. Emma was no longer shut in the danger zone (kitchen) and instead left with the run of the house, which stopped the destructive behaviour immediately. She could choose where she wanted to be (and where she felt safe). Emma chose the top of the stairs and spent her days snoozing happily.

4.7 *Dealing with Destruction by a Dog Left on its Own*

Begin by leaving a radio on, increasing exercise and building up the contents of the toy box, rotating the toys daily. Feed the daily ration of food out of dispensing toys (1.17).

The next step is to alter your routine on leaving the house. Decide where your dog might feel happiest in the house and leave him there as per 4.6 above. Give the dog some sort of treat (biscuit, antler, Kong®) and just go. Always greet the dog when you get back with a smile and brief hello (watch your body language – do not be cross). Do not look around the room for signs of damage until the dog is in the back garden, or in another room with someone else, this is very important. Clear up any mischief while the dog is out of the way, so you do not draw any attention to it. If you have used a Kong® or antler or similar, pick it up and put it away until the next time your dog is left. Allow the dog back in as though nothing has happened. Paint or spray a foul-tasting substance (like Bitter Apple®) on areas the dog is damaging regularly, or block access to that place as this could become habitual.

If your pet still causes damage, try adding a natural calmer to the daily diet. The next step is to plug in a Pet Remedy diffuser or similar, which can be switched on as you leave and off on your return. You can also stop damage by introducing your dog to an indoor crate, also called dens and cages (1.19), but he shouldn't be left in there for hours at a time, and he must be happy about being in the crate before you lock the door.

Everything you try you need to continue for six to eight weeks(ish). Trying one thing one day and then changing because you have not had an instant cure will not work and will cause more confusion and upset to the dog.

4.8 *Chewing for Attention*

A dog that chews to gain attention will look at you while doing it, often with a devilish glint in the eye. Following the steps in 3.9 (Barking for Attention) should make him rethink his actions. As with any attention-seeking behaviour – if he succeeds in making you take notice, he will feel rewarded by it and repeat the exercise ad nauseam.

4.9 *Chewing Car Interiors*

This can be a very expensive habit. It can be avoided by having the dog on a seatbelt harness (using one that has its own clip to slot into the seatbelt slot rather than one where the actual seatbelt is used) but preferably by using a travel crate. He should be restrained for safety reasons anyway. Most damage in this situation occurs when the dog is left alone in the car. It can be caused by the dog feeling bored or becoming over excited because it has seen another dog or cat through the window and attacks the nearest object – the steering wheel – or digs a hole in the seat. Leaving a dog with a nice, tasty antler or stuffed bone or Kong® filled with lip-smacking treats keeps him gainfully employed. Having something really special to work on can reduce interest in what is going on outside in the street or car park. Instead of becoming over-excited, the dog might return quickly to his edible diversion. For more information on car problems, see Chapter 6.

4.10 *Christmas Trees*

Baubles, tinsel, brightly coloured beads and flashing lights can prove to be very tempting for dogs. I recently visited a lady with two young puppies, who spent a substantial part of the time I was there trying to pull down the Christmas tree and throwing the baubles across the living room – dashing out of the tree to chase them as they zoomed along the floor. Puppies and dogs love a good game with decorations, and may just chew them up, unless taught not to. Chocolate tree ornaments will get a dog's nose working as he picks them off one by one – making himself extremely sick in the process (chocolate is poisonous to dogs) and possibly requiring veterinary intervention. My Springer, Parsnip, enjoyed his first ever yuletide a few Christmases ago. He assisted in decorating the tree, running off with a few bits and pieces which we calmly retrieved (we didn't chase him as this would have made it all more of a game). Once the tree was up, we calmly told Parsnip to leave it each time he looked at it or sniffed an outlying branch. We had taught him this by the method outlined in Chapter 10 and we were at the stage where he was responding out of habit, and treats were not required anymore. Parsnip left the tree alone but developed a sneaky way of playing with Pumpkin (the special needs Staffie) closer and closer to the tree and hey presto! Every now and then a bauble was knocked off. The bauble was no longer part of the tree, and in his mind was not something he needed to leave. So, he chomped it up. Once we sussed out his gameplay, we told both dogs to leave the tree as soon as play got close to it and this worked well. We only lost a few little decorations – negligible.

Closing doors to keep dogs away from the tree when they are unsupervised is a straightforward option. It tends to be the younger amongst our canines that raid Christmas trees, and it is something they grow out of quickly. To be on the safe side it is a good idea to always unplug the tree lights when the dog is in the room unattended.

4.11 Electrical Cables

Like us, electricity can be fatal to our pets. Unlike us, they don't realise it. A cable can seem interesting to a young dog

– worthy of a nibble. Rather like a very young child wanting to put his fingers in the plug socket. Coating exposed cables with specially prepared, nasty tasting pet repellent can make the most curious of dogs not want to go there ever again. Be aware that many dogs will like tabasco, mustard and the like, so using a commercial preparation is probably best (Bitter Apple®, Chew Stopper). Blocking access to areas like behind the TV and computer tables (these are places puppies like to go, usually because they get a strong reaction from us) until the puppy is no longer interested in them is probably the best approach. One of the main reasons crates or cages are so popular for young pups is that they remove the possibility of the puppy seriously hurting itself when unattended.

CHAPTER FIVE

The Overactive Pet

5.1 Fidgety Dogs

All young animals are lively – or they should be. However, some dogs appear unable to relax and spend their time constantly on the move, pacing up and down or getting into mischief. When they finally drop down exhausted after doing twenty miles round the living room and garden, they might just have a short nap before starting all over again. Such animals are often thought of as disobedient or, worse still, dominant (1.3 and 1.4).

An overactive dog, as well as pacing around the house, might steal off kitchen surfaces, raid the bin, chew furniture or household items, launch itself repeatedly at its owners, whine continuously and bark at nothing. It will do these things incessantly, with little let-up.

There are dog breeds that naturally have a lot of energy and stamina. When these breeds are crossed, for example a Springer Spaniel with a Dalmatian, the offspring tend to be rather spirited. The difference between an overactive pet and one with natural exuberance is the ability to switch off and relax or focus on one specific task for a period of time. The overactive dog finds this difficult.

Sky, an eight-month-old Boxer-Dalmatian mix, was an exceptionally lively dog. Luckily, she lived with people who could afford to give her lots of time and exercise. The problems they had ranged from Sky barking at them in the evenings, stealing items, and jumping up and grabbing at their hands and clothing. Sky appeared to be overactive, but she wasn't. She was simply getting up to a lot of mischief to gain attention, mainly in the evenings, and because it was all full-on at once her owners felt she was doing it all the time. But Sky did rest and sleep during the day and could lie and chew on an antler for long periods.

She needed a clear communication system in order for her to learn what her owners liked and didn't like. Getting her to understand good behaviour with a clicker (1.6 and 1.7) and bad behaviour with time-outs (1.11) and not giving continual mixed messages (1.14 and 1.15), calmed her down. Clear communication, particularly in a naturally lively dog, is very important. Our pets want to please us, but they also like to please themselves. Most lively dogs are not overactive.

5.2 Emotional Issues

A dog that cannot switch off and gets into everything is not being controlling or dominant or even naughty. These animals can't help the way they are. They are often exhausted, but can't just lie down and take a nap, like a young child that is over-tired. A dog who behaves like this may appear to be very happy (perhaps too happy), but often has a low mood state, usually because of lack of sleep and rest. Instead of becoming grumpy or morose they seek relief by constantly doing something or getting under their owner's feet.

5.3 What Causes a Dog to Become Overactive?

Lack of sleep is a really common cause (1.18). Most dogs that appear overactive are just lively and overbearing. A few are born like it, but in most cases overactive behaviour is created.

With long-term illnesses or recuperation from accidents, the dog can feel a little depressed because of the restrictions imposed on feeding and exercise, and this can turn into overactivity. Living in an emotionally charged house, such as one where the owners decide to divorce, can create emotional problems for a dog (our pets hate arguments and atmospheres). Sudden and profound changes to the dog's living conditions can lower its general mood - for instance, moving to a new house or having a new baby arrive on the scene. Owners dying and people moving out or moving in can all upset the dog's daily life and routine. An owner going back to work after having time off, perhaps through illness, can cause problems. Dogs, like children, require stability and routine. Changing their diet is another common cause.

5.4 Focusing Attention

If there is very little reward in doing something, why bother? This is how overactive pets think. They find it very difficult to learn, or to be taught, because they do not feel success at the level they crave. They get a minor burst of pleasure at getting something right, when it should be major! This makes them unable to concentrate or focus on one thing for very long. Instead of working out a problem calmly, they throw themselves at it and then give up if it doesn't reap instant pleasure.

It is difficult to deal with an overactive dog. We ask them to sit, holding a food treat over their head, and they may just do it. However, even if you give them the treat straight away and shower them with attention and praise, they may not feel sufficiently rewarded to want to repeat the exercise. Within a few minutes they've had enough and gallop around the room looking for their next little burst of pleasure.

Clicker training (1.6 and 1.7) can help here. As far as the dog is concerned, it is all about problem-solving. We give a command – such as the word 'sit' – and if the dog correctly works out what we mean, and does what we want, we reward that success with a click and a food treat. Two rewards – a click followed by a treat – for one task! For a dog that usually feels under-rewarded, double the ration of pleasure can only be of benefit.

Teaching an overactive animal in this way helps it to manage its emotions. We need to ensure the dog feels pleasure properly and can work off its frustration in a positive way. Training your dog to learn good behaviour, using the clicker and following that with a food treat, lifts their mood and helps them to feel happy, contented, and focused. Some natural calmers can also help, as they provide the ingredients for the body to produce additional serotonin, a mood stabilizer (L-Tryptophan and vitamin B6). If you have normal amounts of serotonin you are easily pleased, relaxed, happy and you generally sleep well. Most importantly, you can appreciate success and the rewards associated with it.

An overactive dog often does not have the time to mess about trying to get food out of a food toy. It moves on very quickly to something else that will bring it pleasure. Help it by popping a very special treat under a plastic cup which is easy to knock over or dangling a treat temptingly out of a Kong®. Once they have mastered this, repeat the exercise several times. If they succeed without too much effort at the beginning, they will become keen to scavenge from a toy – this is building on their success and giving them a way of using frustration to their advantage.

Gilbert and Sullivan (Sully) were two black Labrador brothers, completely adorable and totally mad. Gilbert was confident, intelligent and greedy (like most Labs). Sully was not. Sully copied and learned everything from Gilbert, who did his best to obtain maximum rewards for the both of them. Both were active dogs, but Sully was overactive –

especially in any new situation or place. He jumped up at anyone, barked at people out on walks, and could not relax for a minute (our first session was two hours long and Sully was still on the move at the end, whereas Gilbert, after twenty minutes, had settled down to chew a bone and sleep.) They were initially brought to see me because Sully was mounting Gilbert all the time and sucking Gilbert's neck while doing it. This had produced a large sore spot just under Gilbert's left ear. His owners were reluctant to have Sully neutered without seeing if his problem could be cured.

Everything Sully did, especially the mounting and sucking, was to provide himself with the little bursts of pleasure he craved. We added a natural calmer to his diet to make him feel better and calm him down. Both dogs were introduced to the clicker and were fed little treats for sitting, lying down and coming to heel when called (1.6 and 1.7). Their training was done at various times throughout the day as opposed to a set routine. A bleep/spray collar was used to break Sully's list of bad habits, a strong method as Sully's barking at people was seen as very threatening and he was scaring people (1.12 – 1.15). The catalogue of issues tackled systematically, one at a time. Sully's crate time was drastically increased to encourage more sleep (1.18 and 1.19). Ten weeks later Sully had calmed appreciably, Gilbert's neck was almost totally healed, and their owners were able to enjoy both of them again.

5.5 Diet

Diet can affect our dogs in different ways. What's good for one isn't necessarily good for another, so this is another area where we need to keep an open mind. Over the years I have fed dry food, tinned, pouches, trays and raw meat. The food our dog eats may make it overactive. Brain chemicals that keep us stable, happy and calm are manufactured in the body from the food we consume. If a dog is not digesting its food properly, this can affect the body's overall balance. Changing the diet can sort out the animal's activity levels. It is not always wise to go for a low-protein diet as our dogs need the nutrients that proteins provide. On the other hand, high-protein diets will possibly give the pet extra energy, which is not what you want – unless it is a developing youngster where the protein is required for growth. It is not always the case though. I feed my current dogs' raw meat and they are active when they need to be and horizontal the rest of the time.

As with children, food colourants and sugar can be a problem for dogs. If you have a very active beastie it is prudent to go for natural treats with no additives and a pure, premium, dry diet with no coloured bits or raw meat.

5.6 Boredom

Overactivity can also be the result of boredom or lack of exercise. Increasing games and mental stimulation through food toys and training can calm the animal. An extra walk, with a good gallop off-lead, can settle a dog. If you can't let it off the lead, play fetch with a football or frisbee in the garden. It does mean a bit of extra time and input, but it can make the difference between having a whirling dervish in the living room, and a contented pet happy to lie quiet and take a nap.

5.7 Dealing with Overactivity

Evaluate the dog's lifestyle critically. Is he getting enough sleep? (1.18). Does he have adequate exercise? Is the Beastie mentally challenged? (1.6, 1.7 and Chapter 10). Does he understand the house rules? Are we being clear and consistent in our communication? (1.13 to 1.15). These are the areas that may need addressing to make the dog relaxed and happy again. The dog may seem very happy, in which case introducing more walks, feeding in a variety of ways and being consistent in our dealings with it should make it even happier. If the Beastie is truly overactive, making these changes to its daily life should reap positive results in a few short weeks.

CHAPTER SIX

Travelling Problems

6.1 The Need to Travel

You may not have your dog in the car every day, but he'll need to cope with car travel at some point. For instance, visits to the vet, dropping him and picking him up from the kennels and attending training classes. A dog who gets upset in the car may take some time to calm down, which would make obedience training a waste of time, since he'll be anxious throughout the class. Arriving at your destination and having to clean vomit (or worse) out of the car makes you think twice about taking the dog in the first place. A long journey can be a nightmare (and potentially dangerous) if a dog is persistently barking and distracting you from driving. If you do not drive and rely on public transport or taxis, taking him by bus or train may also require some consideration. A dog that is comfortable travelling is often easier to handle at the vet's and settles quickly into a 'holiday home'.

6.2 Emotional Issues

When it comes to travelling, fear, excitement and frustration tend to be the emotions we have to deal with. Who knows what a pet really thinks of a car? A box with windows that constantly twists, turns, stops and starts, while the outside flashes by in an instant. Being in a car can be frightening, especially when you ignore your dog to concentrate on driving. Their anxiety might make them whine or bark for attention. And suffering from motion sickness can be upsetting – for everyone!

By contrast, the dog that often goes on exciting trips in the car can find travelling exhilarating. They can make your ears ring with their constant whining or barking, in anticipation of an adventure. Trying to catch or chase things the other side of the window (and promptly bouncing off it) can be huge fun, or very frustrating. Dogs that are aggressive to people or other dogs generally, may bark or even try to attack them through the car window.

6.3 Dealing with Travel Problems

In my experience dogs that misbehave in the car, or are deeply upset when travelling, can be very difficult to help. There are so many factors that excite, upset, irritate or scare the animal, it can be almost impossible to deal with them all. Perhaps the biggest problem is the fact that once the car's moving, there's not a lot you can do about your dog. The suggestions in this chapter will only help if the Beastie is taken out regularly in the car over a period of weeks and months.

The best way to avoid travelling problems in the first place is by acclimatising a dog to car travel during its early weeks and months. Make good use of safety devices such as harnesses, dog guards and crates (1.19 for introducing your dog to a cage, crate or doggy den).

6.4 Dealing with a Dog that is Poorly or Afraid in the Car

This is a common problem with very young puppies, which only gets worse with time. A dog never grows out of motion sickness or fear, they can only get used to travelling by experiencing it regularly. Going out for short journeys two or three times per day, and extending the trips very gradually, accustoms a dog to being in a moving car. You might begin just by going up and down the drive. It also helps to drive sensibly and not throw the car into corners at speed or leave braking to the last minute. The whole process will take time and patience, and there are no short cuts or fast solutions.

The dog will benefit from being restrained in a car harness, which will stop it being thrown about in the boot or back seat. The harness is similar to a walking harness (some of them double up as both) but has an attachment at the back with a seat belt buckle so it can be clipped into the socket in your car, keeping your dog safe and secure. You can also buy just the strap with the buckle to make use of an existing harness. These keep any mess in one area. Protect the seat if your dog is 'leaky' using old towels with plastic sheeting underneath. It's not just pees and poos you have to consider shielding your car from but extreme drooling and vomit as well. Given this, sometimes a travel crate is the better option…

The dog might also feel more relaxed about travelling if you introduce it to a crate in the house (1.19), and then use the same crate (or a similar one) in the car. If he's upset by the sights whizzing past the window, a thin cloth – one that allows plenty of air to circulate – can be draped over the top of the den to make him feel even safer.

If your dog is afraid in the car, my advice is to ignore it, completely. It sounds harsh, but any response from you, such as giving eye contact or directly trying to comfort the animal, only tells him that he's right to be scared – so his fear increases (8.1 and 8.2). It's easy for the driver of the car to ignore a dog, but passengers also need to help by doing nothing. If you just continue chatting between you as normal, with bright, happy, confident voices, you will signal that the situation is safe. If you keep looking at him, show concern or talk in soothing tones to your dog at this time, you will actually start him really worrying!

A dog can become afraid of the car at any age if it has a bad experience, such as an accident or getting heat stroke from being left in a hot vehicle.

Ziggie, a young Doberman Pinscher, was a model passenger and curled up on a big blanket in the car boot several times a week, often accompanying his owner to work. One frosty morning the car behind, probably going too fast for the conditions, had a braking issue in the ice and rear-ended Ziggie's car. Lights were smashed and the car bumpers were dented, the drivers pride also, I suspect. Luckily, Ziggie wasn't hurt, just shaken up and was given big cuddles and lots of comfort. Following this Ziggie began panting and shaking on just entering the boot, where he had previously sat, quite content. He then started jumping over onto the back seat and trying to get on his owner's lap – whilst he was driving! Installing a dog guard stopped Ziggie trying to escape the boot – he was just too big to go on the back seat – and ignoring him completely by behaving normally swiftly reduced his fears. Learning to be afraid takes but a second, unlearning that fear can take months, years even.

6.5 Does Your Car Suit Your Dog?

Dogs are expensive. People occasionally move to a new house to accommodate their pets, but frequently buy a new vehicle to make travelling easier. When you buy a new car, you need to make sure it's really suitable for your dog. I was once asked for help with a Bull Mastiff, Dylan. His owners had sold their company van and old car on retirement and invested in a large, flashy four-by-four. The dog point-blank refused to get into the new car, although he was perfectly happy in both previous vehicles and this had them perplexed.

Well, we had fun and games with this one. The four-wheel drive was high off the ground, and a Bull Mastiff is not renowned for its ability to hurdle. He tried his very best to get into the car. Despite the promise of several packets of custard creams (his favourite) and drenching us in crumb-infused drool the most he could do was get his front legs up in the boot. He did not have the strength to propel his back legs up as well – although he did put a lot of effort in. He was not afraid of the car; it was just not suited to him. Lifting his back end in manually was the only way of getting him in. The owners did this for a short while, but soon invested in a ramp.

6.6 *Bouncing About*

A dog might bounce about in a car in sheer excitement at going on a journey, leapfrogging from the front to the back or, in the case of some dogs, balancing on the backs of seats. Before the laws changed in the UK regarding travelling with a dog, I had a small car with a parcel shelf and my Doberman, Tosca, would squeeze herself up onto this shelf to bask in the sunshine as we were driving. A friend of mine had a small Terrier that liked to ricochet around the moving car like a bullet. It would only settle and relax on her lap – while she was driving! These situations could cause a fatal accident. If there was a crash, a loose dog in the car, such as Tosca, would not only seriously injure or kill herself, but probably me and my passengers as well. A dog bouncing around is even more dangerous.

No matter how well trained a dog is, you never know for sure what it will do next. A well trained, calm German Shepherd I know decided one day to try and sit on her owner's lap while she was driving down a country lane. Luckily, she was able to stomp on the brakes and narrowly avoided an accident.

Travel crates, seatbelt harnesses and dog guards are there

for our protection as well as the safety of our beloved pets. Use them. Most modern makes of car have their own dog guards that can be properly screwed into place by a garage. Universal guards that you pop in yourself can easily be knocked down by a dog with one paw!

6.7 Barking and Whining in the Car

This is the most common car problem owners see someone like me about. It can be very irritating and distracting to the driver and passengers alike and car journeys tend to be avoided. As with all behaviour problems, we need to deal with the animal's emotional difficulties and then break them of the habit. If securing your dog safely in the car does not help, consider applying some of the methods below.

6.8 Barking at Something through the Car Window

As we have seen in Chapter Three, dogs bark for many reasons, including fear. If a dog is afraid of other dogs, it may bark aggressively to get rid of them – which often seems like a successful strategy in a car, as it's often moving away, or the dog is walking on by (9.3 and 9.21). A dog may feel frustrated in the car, because he desperately wants to get at another dog or person he can see – and he vents his emotions through barking, which makes him feel better. Or maybe the dog barks just to let his owners know there are strangers around.

In all these situations, the dog finds barking rewarding. Feeding him treats to distract him from what is going on outside can make matters worse, unless your timing is impeccable. Your dog may stop barking to get his treat, but he might believe you are rewarding him for what he's just done. That could make him bark even more in the hope of greater rewards. It is better to provide him with a tasty stuffed bone or Kong® that will keep him so busy he won't even bother to look outside (4.9 Chewing Car Interiors). The Kong® or bone needs to be given to the dog before it starts barking.

For a dog that is not easily distracted using food, take the fun out of barking and make the dog rethink its actions using your 'leave it' command (10.12), 'enough' if you use it at home (3.14) or suggestions from 1.12 – 1.15. If you are able to take a passenger with you in the car each time, then a water-squirter or Pet Corrector™ may suffice, carefully following the advice in Chapter 1 on how to introduce a failure signal and not forgetting to ignore the dog for at least thirty seconds afterwards as per 1.14 Mixed Messages and 1.15 The Thirty Second Rule.

A bleep/spray collar may be more useful for the very excited dog, although as someone has to activate the remote control you will still need the help of a passenger. But before you scrabble back the pages and begin strategizing your battle plan don't forget a covered crate with a tasty bone in can take away all the triggers that start the dog barking in the first place.

Jake, a seven-year-old Weimaraner, used to pound at the boot window of the car whenever he saw other animals, especially dogs and cats, and he would bark for all he was worth. He made the car rock! Most of the journeys his owner took with him were local – so Jake had many opportunities to express himself. Apart from this, Jake was well-behaved in other places and was very sociable and friendly towards other dogs (but not cats).

We advised giving Jake a bone stuffed with corned beef and dog treats. This special indulgence was saved for the car, to keep its value to Jake high. As soon as his owner lifted the car boot, Jake would salivate in anticipation of his bone. This kept him busy when the car was moving, but when the car stopped Jake would stop worrying at the toy. A water squirter had to be used to stop him pouncing at the window and barking. This quickly taught him that playing with his bone was a more profitable occupation.

6.9 Dealing with a Dog Barking for Attention in the Car

These guys are easy to spot as they stare at you the whole time they are barking (3.9 Barking for Attention). As with all attention-seeking problems, if you give the dog what he wants – a look, a word or a stroke – then he will continue doing whatever he was doing because it works. Shouting over your shoulder at a barking attention seeker on the back seat will not help! This is where you definitely need a cure that the dog won't associate with you. Squirting water at him could be seen as giving him attention, so could the 'leave it' or enough' commands, which may be enough to keep him barking, regardless of the effects. If you have tried a covered travel crate with a bone in it, and it hasn't helped and you really cannot ignore the racket your dog is making, a bleep/spray remote control collar coupled with ignoring him completely is perhaps the next step (1.12 – 1.15).

Rosie, a Cocker Spaniel, loved nothing more than being with her owner. She often barked when she was ignored, but when she did it in the car her owner couldn't stand the noise. When the owner began a new relationship with someone who lived miles away, it became impossible to avoid the problem any longer. Rosie had to get used to being in the car. She was given nice chews and a stuffed Kong® in the boot. She ignored these – so a bleep/spray collar was deployed. Rosie quickly learned that she should not bark when she had this collar on, and she wears it to this day even though the batteries no longer work. Just having it on is enough to stop her.

6.10 *Rhythmical Barking in the Car*

The rhythmical barker (bark then pause, bark then pause) is doing this to help him cope (3.5). He may feel afraid or anxious. His bark releases some 'happy chemicals' in the brain, making him feel temporarily better. As with all fear and anxiety issues, a natural calmer in his food may be useful. In more extreme situations, medication from the vet may be required.

A rescued Terrier called Hamish had many behavioural problems, one of which was his steady but regular bark when in the car. The vet prescribed some medicine to be used for a short while to help Hamish get over his anxiety. This relaxed Hamish, who was also introduced to a travel crate (1.19), which he came to see as a place of safety. Hamish soon stopped barking and was weaned off the strong medication after a few weeks. A dietary supplement was added to his food to keep him buoyant and able to deal with life.

6.11 *Excitement Barking*

Dogs have an uncanny knack of knowing where they are going. Some become excited as the car turns into a certain street, because it leads to their favourite park or the woods. Others find the prospect of returning home thrilling and start shouting. Being a very clever species, taking different routes home or to special places will not fool a dog for long. Hannah, my German Shepherd, went crazy in the back of the car if we headed for the local woods. I tried using other roads that frankly looked the same to me, but she knew! If the dog only barks for a few minutes, this may not be a big issue. But if he barks for the whole journey, convinced he is going somewhere exciting, you may have to do something about it.

Barking makes a dog feel happier, and the happier he

feels, the more likely he is to bark, and so it goes on. If strapping him in, confining him to a covered or open crate, and offering tasty bones and Kongs® does not help, and you have tried 'leave it' (10.12) or 'enough' (3.14) to no avail, then you may have to use a water squirter or one of the other failure signals in Chapter 1 (1.12 – 1.15). However, sometimes this problem can be successfully dealt with by simply popping on a head collar, like a Gentle Leader.

Piglet, a head-strong Red Lakeland Terrier, became exhilarated at the prospect of going in the car to the point he tried to attack the windscreen wipers. Placing a Gentle Leader (10.7) on him just for the journey calmed him to the point of nodding off to sleep...

6.12 The Frustrated Barker

This is the most difficult of all emotions to deal with. Frustrated dogs don't respond well to failure signals – the signal may only increase the frustration and make the dog bark louder. It can be difficult to recognise a frustrated barker; one tell-tale sign is the intensity of the bark, with lots of effort being put into each woof. Often the frustrated dog barks at nothing – not at you nor anything outside. The dog will also become generally agitated if he doesn't get what he wants straightaway. A frustrated pet can be overactive and difficult to train or focus (see Chapters 5 and 10).

It's best to deal first with the dog's general frustration, and then tackle the barking in the car. Problem-solving exercises like clicker training can really help (1.7). Getting a dog to cope with its frustration by playing with a Kong® stuffed with treats, can improve mood.

Jessie, an English Bull Terrier, had a big bark and made sure everyone he travelled with knew about it. He was strapped into the back seat of the vehicle on a car harness. This was a major feat, because whenever Jessie saw the car harness he began to leap about and bark. He behaved the same way if his dinner wasn't prepared quickly enough, if he could smell food in the kitchen, or if he wasn't getting fed while his owners were eating. We tackled his general frustration first, by feeding him using food toys, and by using a clicker to train him to sit, lie down, leave it and stay. By adding a mood-lifting supplement to his daily diet and increasing the amount of exercise he got in the garden and local park, we helped Jessie become calmer and less agitated. Only then did we approach his car problem, using a yummy bone (not a Kong® due to the strength of his jaws) to provide a delicious alternative to barking.

6.13 The Chase Instinct and the Car Window

Certain breeds of dog limit themselves to the eye, stalk, chase part of the hunting sequence. Collies and German Shepherd dogs are among the numerous 'herders' who love nothing better than chasing a moving target. But the chase instinct can also be taught, regardless of breed. When you train a dog to fetch, you are effectively teaching it to chase a moving target.

Chasing something that runs by a window can be immense fun, but through a car window it's fantastic! The target is moving so much faster, keeping the chaser primed and ready for speedy action. Bouncing off the windows can add to the pleasure, as it gives contact (albeit with glass) at the end of the eye, stalk, chase sequence.

In mild cases, the dog can be taught using a 'leave it' command (10.12) to cease and desist. The 'enough' command (3.14) might just do the trick if you use it at home. But where dogs are driven to chase obsessively, a noise signifying bad behaviour will have no impact at all. A covered crate, or car sunshades so the dog cannot see out of the car windows, will stop him; if he can't see the targets, he won't try and chase them. If your car is not big enough for a doggy den, then tethering the dog on a very short lead in the rear foot well can work just as well (tether to the metal fixtures underneath the front seats). The dog should not have enough lead to strangle itself or jump up onto the rear seat, and you must use a proper car harness, not a collar and lead for safety reasons. Using this technique, the dog cannot see out of windows and has limited freedom of movement.

Roger, a crossbreed, ran at everything he could see out of the rear window of his owner's van. He bounced off the windows, leaving them covered in dog snot. The van had no real space for a doggy den as it was often full of tools, so Roger was tied to the front passenger seat in the foot well, using a harness. His owner could see him, but Roger could not see out of the vehicle – a simple and effective solution.

6.14 Refusing to Get in the Car

A little dog is easy to get into a car – if it won't jump, you can lift it up. However, many dogs are too big to be manhandled. A dog may refuse to jump into the car for many reasons – perhaps because it is frightened or anxious or, as with Dylan, the Bull Mastiff in 6.5, because it simply can't make it. Some dogs are fine with a car they are used to but can become reluctant to get into a new car. I once spent a fascinating afternoon with a giant schnauzer, Bruno, who didn't like change. Bruno was a drama queen. He was such a creature of habit, any alterations to his daily routine caused problems. Moving to a new house had him in a real tizzy for a while, and the arrival of a new car sent him into an emotional spin.

The car was a low-slung estate, purchased primarily so he could get in and out easily and had enough space to spread himself. On approaching the back of the car, Bruno dug his feet into the ground, rejecting the invitation to get in. Moving a dog of this size is no mean feat if he says no! To motivate him, goodies were produced from the kitchen, but he turned up his nose at them. He could be bought – we just had to find out what by. Home-baked cheese straws were the prize he settled for. One was held about a foot in front of Bruno's nose. He had to step forward to take it. Another one was dangled, temptingly just out of reach at the back of the car. Bruno reluctantly stepped forward to take it, whereupon another cheese straw appeared and was put in the boot of the car, just far enough in for Bruno to have to put his head inside. This continued until Bruno had got both front feet in the boot and was straining forward to get at the cheese straws. Then I clambered in (it was a big boot and had the back seats down). From this position I could lay out a feast of cheese straws and show Bruno there was nothing to be worried about. He finally jumped in and ate the lot. We got him out after a few minutes, then stood at the back of the car and threw in a cheese straw. Bruno went straight in after it and there has been no car refusal since.

Your car boot may not always be suitable for your dog but getting him to jump up onto the back seat can be tricky. Try sitting yourself on the back seat, as far away from the door as you can get, calling the dog in while waving suitable goodies. Make a path of treats, so the dog eats the first one easily but has to get inside the car to get the rest. For dogs that ignore all your attempts, open both back doors, so that the dog has a way out as well as a way in. Throw treats and toys into the car, or through the car. Make a game out of it. Only close the doors with the dog inside when he is happy getting in and out.

6.15 Refusing to Get Out of the Car

This is not quite as common as refusing to get in. Some dogs have a love affair with cars and will jump into any vehicle if a door or boot is open. Once in, they don't want to get out.

Coax the dog out with a treat or toy and a happy voice. If the dog comes to you when it is called – call it.

If neither of these techniques work, you will have to pull the dog out. Pulling by the collar (or front legs) can seriously hurt a dog. Put a standard walking harness on and clip a lead to it. This allows you a little more licence in gradually forcing the dog out. Pull slowly and steadily – avoid yanking. If a dog regularly repeats this behaviour, keep the harness on him until the habit is broken. Saying something like, 'out you get' at the same time gives the dog a phrase he can learn – so he knows what you want him to do.

CHAPTER SEVEN

Chasing

7.1 Why Our Dogs Love to Chase

Dogs are natural born hunters – or at least their ancestors were. The chase instinct is still very strong in them, although now usually exercised through play. We encourage this activity through games with toys, because it is a wonderful way of exercising and mentally stimulating our dogs. Dogs pursue something because they are attracted to the way it moves and their behaviour varies according to breed, but chasing is an important component for most. For those that do not chase naturally, we often teach them to run after a moving target through the game of fetch (10.14).

Although chasing is a totally natural part of our dogs' lives, it is what and when they choose to chase that can cause difficulties.

7.2 Emotional Issues

Reward – huge amounts of it – is the name of the game with chase behaviour. Dogs chase when they feel threatened, or feel their territory is in danger. The outcome is one big buzz at successfully seeing off the intruder. A dog chomping away on a bone may physically (and sometimes menacingly) chase off another interested party. Chasing can be used as an act of self-defence, or defence of something it values. It is a big act of bravado that often pays off.

Some dogs chase to gain attention – usually from other dogs – if they are being ignored. This attempt at play is often driven by mild feelings of frustration, which can make the dog overreact and be a little too forceful with the other animal. The pursued dog may be overawed by this attention and react defensively – leading to pistols at dawn!

When a dog is hunting, its emotions are pure pleasure. They are not angry, frustrated or aggressive, but simply following instinct, and having the time of their lives!

7.3 Chasing Cars, Buses and Lorries

Dogs tend to chase vehicles because they have been a little spooked by them at some point. Trolling along the street, having a nice quiet walk with its owner, the young dog is happy sniffing and taking in the sights. Suddenly a car or lorry comes hurtling past, making the dog jump and pull back in fright. Its concerned owner bends over the shaking creature and whispers a few comforting words or picks it up. The youngster has been seriously scared, and knows its reaction was appropriate because its owner rewarded it by making a fuss (8.1 – 8.3). This only needs to happen once for a dog to learn that passing vehicles are something to be worried about. Some dogs will carry on being scared and always pull away slightly or hide behind their owner. Braver dogs take it upon themselves to despatch the scary truck by chasing it off in an act of total daring. The reward for this activity is massive as the dog enjoys total success – without, of course, realising that the truck was never going to stop anyway.

This problem is potentially dangerous to the dog, dog owner and road users. A vehicle-chaser when off the lead may disappear into the distance while pursuing his target. The chaser's owner needs to be extra vigilant even when the dog is on the lead, as he can give a sudden, sharp pull towards a car that could injure his owner or catch them off balance, so the animal gets into the road and causes an accident.

7.4 Dealing with a Vehicle Chaser

The more obsessed a dog is with chasing cars, the harder it is to deal with. Their obsession grows over time, so it's important to deal with it as soon as it starts to occur. Offer the dog a treat or a toy that he will rate more highly than the reward he gets from chasing. Keeping the treat in your hand, wave it under his nose just before the vehicle passes and before he starts to chase. Tease the dog with the treat until the car has gone, and if he hasn't attempted to go after it, give him his reward. Don't be tempted to keep the treat for the next car. A dog will quickly pick up on this and will simply go for whatever reward is most easily available – which may be chasing the car. It sometimes helps to use a treat that is smelly – cheese or sausage for example – as its smell will register quickly with the dog. Squeaky toys are also good for getting a dog's attention, though he may need to be given the toy for a minute to play with, which isn't practical if there are lots of cars about. Once you have the dog's attention, use the treat or toy to get him to sit (10.4).

A dog can be easily distracted by playing tuggy with a rope toy while you walk. If you keep the game going and your dog is enjoying it, he will want to go on playing regardless of how many vehicles pass. Tuggy is all about pulling harder and harder, and the longer it goes on the more effort a dog puts in. This is a fun method that can make a walk more enjoyable for a dog. It can, though, be very tiring on the arms!

A chaser has to be taught that there is no reward in dashing off. With a Pet Corrector™ or water-squirter, having followed the introduction method in 1.12, give your warning signal just as the dog is about to chase, and follow through with the spray only if needed (don't forget to ignore for thirty seconds as per 1.14). This can work well if he's on a lead. Dogs that chase when on and off the lead can be helped using the bleep/spray collar, which works at a distance. But it's very important to train them on the lead first, so the dog knows what the bleep means. If he doesn't grasp what the bleep will lead to, he may be out of range before you have had an opportunity to activate the spray. Running into the wind at speed can direct the spray away from the dog, so he won't feel it at all. It is crucial the dog learns that a bleep signifies that chasing in this situation is bad behaviour. It also helps if you teach him to come back when called as soon as possible (10.8 and 10.9).

Jazz was a large and very fast Lurcher who loved to chase farm vehicles. He would race across three fields to get to his chosen quarry. Being so fast, a bleep/spray collar had no effect until he was taught what the bleep meant. We put a delicious sandwich in the kitchen and walked out of the room. In no time at all we heard the tell-tale sound of paws on the work surface. Jazz was bleeped and then sprayed for trying to get at something he knew he shouldn't have. Additional encounters with forbidden fruits, in the living room and elsewhere, taught Jazz exactly what the bleep was about. On the next walk, Jazz chose to ignore the tractor in the next field as soon as he heard the 'beep beep' sound from his collar.

Once the dog has learned that chasing is no fun, you can begin rewarding good behaviour by using a clicker and giving treats (1.7) for good responses to training. This replaces the fun the dog is losing out on, keeps him focused on his owner, and reinforces lead and coming-when-called training.

Walking a dog on a head collar instead of a neck collar or harness can also help. The head collar gives you much more control of a dog because it can't use its whole bodyweight to resist you. Finger-tip control of the head allows you to turn the dog away from a car or hold him easily so he can't zoom off, though it won't stop him wanting to.

Extender leads allow a dog freedom, without him being free. If a dog is an avid chaser, then using one of these to keep control of the animal in a field or park is a good compromise. Using them in the street is not a good idea, in case it breaks, or you don't lock it into place properly. Care is needed though, as the dog can exert phenomenal pull on the lead if they run to the end of it, which can injure both dog and owner.

7.5 Chasing Cyclists and Joggers

The stealth and speed with which a cyclist or jogger approaches on a path can make you jump. If you fail to hear them approaching from behind, you can get a shock when they are suddenly upon you. It's the same with dogs, except they may go into self-defence mode, bark at the stranger and chase him off. The success the dog feels from doing this, spurs him on to do it again next time – only he probably won't wait to be surprised again. Instead, he'll keep a wary eye and ear out for the cyclist or jogger and try and head them off at the pass. Any shouting or gesticulating by the cyclist or jogger only raises the stakes and fuels the dog's excitement. If the jogger or cyclist stays still, the dog may stop long enough to be called to heel by its owner, but not surprisingly this doesn't happen often! A dog in full flight after a moving target can nip or bite in its excitement (a nip is a little bite using the small front teeth only).

A cyclist may be knocked off his bike by an over-friendly dog who is enthusiastic in his greetings. Joggers can be tripped up by dogs or knocked sideways if they jump up at them. These situations are serious. People who are scared by a dog may make a formal complaint. Being run down by a dog is also frightening, and the fear is worse if the owner is calling the dog to no avail, which makes it look as if the animal is out of control.

7.6 Dealing with People Chasers

My favourite approach to this is 'leave it' training and this is what I use daily on my walks. Leave that crisp packet, leave that poo, leave that dog, leave that jogger. By teaching this (10.12) it is easily transferrable onto pretty much anything.

Take a critical look at how much attention your dog gets on a walk. Do you play with him enough, or leave him to amuse himself? You can often distract a dog from chasing a jogger by playing fetch with something he can chase without getting into trouble. Take some food treats on your walk and give your dog tasks to do like wait, sit, down, leave it and stay so he is not just entertaining himself (Chapter 10). Giving a dog a reason to pay attention to you stops him mentally wandering off and as a nice side effect the dog's training improves. Don't always take the same old ball or toy with you – try a Frisbee or a football or something squeaky instead. Many dogs like a ball that they can squish in their mouths – like a tennis ball. They don't last long – not like a solid hard ball – but dogs prefer them. It is a myth that chasers should not be allowed to play fetch because it encourages them to chase people and other unsuitable things. Dogs can tell the difference between a person and a toy. They can also learn that one should not be chased while the other is perfectly acceptable. Keep these fetch sessions a reasonable length, 10 minutes perhaps, so we don't wear out their bodies with all the running, jumping and twisting.

The dog that cannot be distracted by games needs to learn that chasing is not good. It is wise to keep him on an extender lead in wide open spaces until all signs of chasing have disappeared. However, a clever chaser may not chase at all when on the lead and fool you into thinking he's cured! One way to sort him out is to enlist the help of a tolerant friend who doesn't mind being chased when the dog is loose. Setting the scene in this way allows you to work on the problem without the risk of prosecution or abuse.

Gizmo, a Collie crossed with a Terrier, loved to chase joggers in the park. When he caught up with them, which was in no time at all, he would jump up in excitement, sometimes catching their clothing in his teeth. Although vigilant on walks, Gizmo's owner was often caught out and subjected to the angry ranting of irate fitness fanatics. One fine day, Gizmo went too far. Instead of a piece of shorts, he got a sliver of flesh. The jogger was understandably peeved, and the local constabulary called on Gizmo's owner. 'Sort it or shoot it' was the fundamental message.

Keeping Gizmo on an extender lead initially, his owner used a bleep/spray collar (1.2 and 1.4) to teach him that chasing joggers was a very, very bad idea. For every jogger Gizmo did not attempt to chase, he was given a squeaky toy with a tail to capture and 'kill' (Terriers are very tuned into squeaks). If the owners had taught Gizmo to leave it as a puppy (10.12) the whole situation could easily have been avoided.

If all else fails don't let the dog off his lead.

7.7 Chasing Livestock and Other Animals

Dogs do get shot chasing livestock and in the UK the farmer, legally, has every right to do so. In fact, the dog does not have to be chasing the sheep or cattle – being off lead can be enough. A few years ago, a chap was out jogging with his two German Shepherd dogs as usual. Going through a field of sheep, one dog either side of him, he heard two bangs.

Both dogs dropped to the floor. One was killed outright, the other so severely injured it was put to sleep. The guy was lucky not to have been shot himself. The police were called but he had no redress.

It's not worth it. Even if a dog is superbly behaved (as these two dogs were), don't take the chance. If there is livestock anywhere along your daily walk, put the dog on the lead *before* you get there. Unclip the lead again when you are well and truly past. A dog can decide to chase at any moment – we cannot fully predict their next move – and it is totally normal for *them!* I have been called hundreds of times to help with livestock chasing problems – there is no problem if the dog is restrained.

Stopping dogs from chasing cats, squirrels and other furry creatures is also fraught with difficulty. If the dog is chasing the squirrel in the absence of anything else to do, a water-squirter or a bleep/spray collar (1.12) *might* work. Leave it training (10.12) would be a definite *possibility*. As with 7.6 above, working on the problem using an extender lead and suitably interesting toys can reap good results. If the dog is chasing because it is hunting – then this is a different ball game altogether. The only real way to stop this instinctive behaviour is by physically restraining the dog.

7.8 Chasing and Body-Slamming Other Dogs

The motivation for some dogs to play with others can be very strong. If ignored, the dog can become frustrated. Rather like a child in the playground that pinches and punches because no one wants to play with him, the dog can start to behave like a lout – chasing down his victim and literally slamming into him, bowling him over. Not many dogs want to play after that! Not many owners want their dog to play after that sort of experience either. So, Billy No Mates is left feeling even more frustrated until the next victim arrives.

The owner of a dog like this can feel equally annoyed. After all, the dog only wants to play – he's just a little rough around the edges. But the truth is, a victim of body-slamming can develop behaviour issues of its own and begin to feel threatened or scared by other dogs. It can even be seriously injured.

7.9 Dealing with a Body-Slammer

There are two basic factors here – taking away the dog's frustration at having no one to play with and getting rid of the habit. One of the quickest ways of teaching the dog not to behave like this is to mix him with lots of dogs on a regular basis. Training clubs, agility or fly ball gatherings – they all introduce a dog to others in a controlled environment. Walking your dog out with other owners and their dogs, will give him some doggie friends, reducing the need to interfere with new dogs on a walk. Keeping your dog on a lead or extender lead when introducing him to an unknown dog will reduce the initial excitement. Once the dogs have sniffed each other and walked along for a while calmly, you can usually let them off the lead to play.

Bessie, a lively chocolate Labrador, bowled over every dog she met. Some were fine about it and still played with her, making her behaviour rewarding and ensuring she repeated it. Other dogs growled or ran away. Bessie's basic training was excellent; she would come back to her owner on hearing two pips of a whistle, which was blown whenever her owner spotted a new dog. Bessie was rewarded for this with a treat and popped on the lead. Introduced to the new dog, still on her lead, Bessie was calm, even a little bashful. When she was let off after a few minutes of walking, Bessie approached the stranger with confidence and played in a lady-like fashion. After a few weeks it was unnecessary to put her on the lead, as her advances to other dogs were no longer so rough.

7.10 Chasing Children and Other Family Members

There can be a superb rapport between dogs and kids. Running around the garden chasing a squealing child can be great fun – but sometimes the dog can become over-excited and start nipping the child, as it might if it was playing with another dog. This is not aggression or being nasty, but that's what it can feel like to the child – it hurts and even leaves small bruises. Children don't really understand about keeping dogs calm, so it's up to adults to intervene and control the types of games they play. Encouraging a dog to chase a child is asking for trouble, even if it is just fun. Dogs often don't know where to draw the line.

Fetch is a good game to encourage a child to play with a dog (see 10.14); throwing a Frisbee, rope toy, Kong® or ball are all suitable. So is kicking a football for the dog to bring back; it encourages the dog to chase something other than the child! Teaching children at an early age how to get the dog to sit or lie down will help them calm a dog that is going over the top. A dog can become highly charged if play is too rough or exciting.

7.11 Play Fighting, Wrestling or Rough-housing a Dog

Dogs don't always know when to stop playing. If you chase your dog and wrestle him to the floor, then let him do the same to you, you shouldn't be surprised if he uses his teeth to hold onto you. As his bites get harder, you become cross and tell him off. In his 'wild' state he may read this wrong, believe the game has been raised to another level, and launch himself at you.

If you play rough with a puppy you will never stop the play biting.

A timid dog can feel very threatened by this type of game, become scared of his owner and use aggression to protect himself (9.5). There are few dogs who really understand that this is just a game, and who have the emotional control to switch the excitement on and off the way we do!

Dax, a Staffordshire Bull Terrier, felt very threatened by his male owner. But instead of becoming aggressive towards him, Dax began to pee in the house whenever his 'dad' was home. Dad thought Dax needed toughening up to get over his timidity and roughed him up a lot – just in play. He would creep up behind the dog and suddenly pick him up and throw him onto his back. Applying pressure to Dax's chest and stomach he would wriggle the dog about on the floor. As Dax struggled free, Dad would slap him (gently) around the body and face to try and get him to fight back. We had to teach Dad to stop this type of game and change it to a game of tuggy (which Staffordshire's adore). This soon cured the toilet problem and increased the bond between dog and owner.

If a dog's behaviour is getting over the top or feels threatened by this type of game, the only real solution is to stop playing it and do something else instead.

7.12 Chasing Our Dogs

Chasing a dog is one of the quickest ways of undoing all that training you did to get it to come when called. Calling a dog and then chasing it if it doesn't respond turns the whole situation into a wonderful game. For more information on coming when called check out 10.8 and 10.9.

CHAPTER EIGHT

Phobias and Other Weird Stuff

8.1 Phobias

A phobia is excessive fear or panic over something, usually something very specific. Many people are frightened of heights, spiders or enclosed spaces, for example. There is often no real explanation for the fear, but it is nonetheless all-consuming. I join the ranks of 'arachnophobes' (fear of spiders). There are certain 'no go' areas at home and in the garden for me. I would never walk-through dense foliage, go into a garden shed or venture to climb into the attic. I can spot a spider at a great distance and have a deep suspicion of anything small that moves quickly. On entering any room, my reflex reaction is to scan the room swiftly, checking for signs of life in dark corners. I no longer do this consciously. When I see a spider, I freeze and cannot take my eyes off it. I can become very angry if no one takes me seriously about getting rid of it. My husband knows the 'spider' scream and comes to my rescue straightaway – having had his head bitten off a few times for not reacting to my distress quickly enough in the past. It is a silly fear – and I know it! But I cannot help the way I feel. Neither can I control the fear – it is out of my hands. When I was very young there was a large spider in my bedroom. My brother came to help and told me he had killed it. Walking back into what I now considered as a safe area, I was deeply shocked to see the spider (it was so large you could count the hairs on its eyebrows) coming at me from under my bed. I have never fully trusted my brother since.

It is very hard, once a phobia has been acquired, to reason it away – and we're talking about humans with advanced thought processes and communication skills. Dealing with a phobic dog is much harder. Dogs can become fearful of anything. Common phobias are loud bangs (fireworks, crow-scarers, guns), thunder and flies. I have also come across dogs with a profound fear of hoovers, drills, children, water, rain, wind, squeaky toys, dolls, motorbikes, cars, lorries, hi-vis jackets, cigarette packets, food sizzling in a frying pan, radios and televisions to name a few.

8.2 Emotional Issues Involved with Phobias

Intense fear can lead to panic. There are many changes that occur within the body at times of extreme fear – these in themselves can be frightening to a dog and can increase the panic. These changes, which include a fast heartbeat and quickened breathing rate, occur so that you can save yourself by running away or fighting for your life.

As with anything unpleasant, when the panic is over, we feel huge relief. Relief is very rewarding. A dog running from something scary feels great – because it has survived – and huge amounts of happy chemicals are released, giving the dog a buzz. This is why people do bungee jumps and other dangerous sports – surviving a jump gives a feeling of total euphoria.

A seriously scared dog will run away or fight if cornered but can also scratch and dig - trying to find an escape - if they are enclosed. Losing toilet control can also indicate panic.

8.3 *How We Can Help*

Trying to deal with a phobic dog involves vast problems. If you try comforting, you will increase the fear because the dog realises you are taking it seriously. Simply by acknowledging the dog's fear you indicate it is right to be afraid. On the other hand, it goes against our nature to ignore an animal in distress. Your dog depends on you for everything, yet with a phobia you may be at a loss to know what help you should give. The dog may deal with the fear himself by running away and will feel hugely rewarded having escaped. Yet many of the things that panic dogs are difficult or impossible to avoid, like thunder.

The single most important thing you can do is to ignore your dog completely. I hear your sharp intake of breath, but it's true. Do not look at him, speak to him or about him and don't touch. This can be aided by some of the ideas below, but if you ignore this one rule you are unlikely to change anything.

Keeping the dog calm helps. You can use a calming dietary additive to relax the animal and plug-in diffusers available from pet shops and veterinary surgeons, which should help him cope better with difficult situations. Thundershirts™ were invented for this, I believe. You may have to use these aids for many months, as the dog may be exposed to its phobia at any time. Provide a safe area in the house that the dog can get to whenever it needs to, such as a crate or secluded area. If the dog likes to go upstairs and get underneath the bed when it is scared, then this is the place it feels safest. Leave well alone and don't try to communicate with him or get him out from the hidey hole, just allow him to cope in his own way. Some dogs stare out of windows or at walls when they are scared. Don't interrupt this – it is a coping strategy and shows progress. For dogs with noise phobias, CDs of noises such as fireworks and thunder can be played at a low volume. If you increase the volume very slowly (maybe one notch per week) and play the CD often, the dog may get used to it and become less fearful as this can reduce the shock. It is important to remember, though, that a thunderstorm arrives with full atmospheric effects and the noise comes from everywhere. It's not the same on a stereo – only regular exposure to the real thing will help a dog become accustomed to the sound without being afraid.

Tilly, a medium-sized crossbreed, was adopted by her owner. Although a little nervous at first, Tilly slipped into a routine with her new owners within a few weeks. On New Year's Eve many loud fireworks were let off and they went on for several hours. Each bang sent Tilly darting around the room, looking for a place to hide. As the night progressed and the volume increased, Tilly's owners tried to comfort her with lots of reassuring words and cuddles. This compounded Tilly's fear, and by the end of the evening she was literally sitting on her owners' heads at the back of the sofa, making it difficult for them to move. Tilly was panting, shaking, pacing and drooling. She would not go outside to toilet nor would she eat or drink.

Tilly grew progressively worse throughout the evening due to the intensity of the firework display and her owners' reactions. Although well-intentioned, the cuddles and attention given to Tilly confirmed to her that she was right to be afraid, and also made her behaviour very successful. The next day Tilly started to jump at every sudden noise. By ignoring Tilly completely, over many months, and not acknowledging that anything was happening, Tilly stopped being jittery and life returned to normal. This sounds easy but it strains every sinew of humanity as it goes very much against our nature.

It is sensible to keep a dog with a serious noise phobia on the lead when walking him. It may only take one bang for the dog to run all the way home on his own.

8.4 *Eating Strange Things*

Dogs will have a nibble at many different things, particularly when they are young. Like young children everything is looked at, sniffed, touched and then popped in the mouth. It is not uncommon for our dogs to have a nosh at tissues, chew up paper and mess around a bit with cotton wool. But when an animal eats something that cannot pass through its system, then it's in trouble. At my dog training school, we had to remove all the small toys from the toybox because a Dalmatian ate a small Kong®, designed for little dogs. It picked it up, rolled it around its mouth for a few seconds and as we all looked on, aghast, swallowed it. The dog was taken straight away to have the Kong® surgically removed (I never got it back!).

I have seen dogs that have ingested half the linoleum from the kitchen floor and many other items besides, which owners hadn't realised were 'missing'. One such dog, a Labrador called Teal, ate stones among other things. She had four operations to remove items from her stomach, one of which was a metal paperweight, four-and-a-half centimetres in diameter and very, very heavy. When I held it in my hand, I could not believe a dog had swallowed it.

Dogs eat strange things for many reasons. If a dog has chewed something up when his owner was out, something he has been punished for, he may eat the evidence. A dog, having stolen something from under our noses, may swallow it quickly as we try and retrieve it. We humans do not own the rights to comfort eating. An unhappy dog may eat whatever is there, because eating helps it to feel better. And of course, he eats the item – just because it is there!

8.5 Dealing with Dogs Eating Strange Items (Pica)

For serious situations where the dog is eating things that could cause sickness or even death, you need to take precautionary measures. Introduce the dog to a crate (1.19) and when you're not there to supervise, place your dog in his crate. Teach leave it as suggested in 10.12 as this can really help. Judicious use of a muzzle will stop your dog eating forbidden goods out on walks or in the garden. If needed, use a device like a bleep/spray collar (1.12) to teach your dog to be wary of dangerous items (the collar can be attached to an item, for instance a plant, and the dog may think the plant is a risky venture).

Mollie, a bouncy Springer Spaniel, was obsessed with eating stones and rubbish out on walks. Once she had an item in her mouth, any attempt to remove it made her swallow straightaway. Using an open-faced muzzle (9.7), one we could poke treats through, we taught Mollie to leave. This was practiced out on walks for approximately twelve weeks by which time she was exceptional at it. By swapping Mollies toys for treats and then giving them straight back to her she was taught to drop items when asked. Then it was time for Mollie to walk muzzle free.

8.6 When a Dog Licks or Grooms Itself Sore

Licking is a normal part of grooming and keeping clean, but sometimes a dog will lick itself sore, even to the point of bleeding. With excessive hair loss (or complete baldness) in the target area, an infection can set in. A dog can suddenly develop this behaviour at any time in its life. The main reasons for obsessive licking are pain, discomfort or itching, however anxiety, stress, frustration or boredom can also be a factor.

A knock or bump can cause a small unseen injury. This

can hurt for a while or a small infection can develop, causing the area to tingle. This makes the dog lick it. A skin irritation caused by allergy or infestation will make the dog pay marked attention to the foot, tail or body. For any problem with excessive grooming, a thorough veterinary check-up is needed. Once all bodily issues have been ruled out, then attention can be turned to the emotional cause.

8.7 Emotional Issues – Licking Problems

The repetitive action of licking can be gratifying. Scratching an itch is immensely pleasurable. If you have ever suffered from eczema or dermatitis or been bitten by a mosquito, scratching the area becomes more delightful the harder you do it. The pain from the wound you are creating does not creep in until the incredible pleasure chemicals released by your brain lose their effect. Then it hurts. Some dogs lick areas because of the pleasure it once afforded them. Such habits are easy to acquire and difficult to break.

Finding comfort in the action of grooming, a dog may feel relief from anxiety, frustration or stress through performing the action again and again, until the area is swollen, sore and hairless. Some dogs do it to gain our attention – and feel successful and rewarded because we show concern.

8.8 Dealing with Excessive Licking or Grooming

Finding out why a dog feels the need to lick itself all the time can be difficult. If there has been a medical condition, this may have returned (check with the vet) – or it may be an obsessive habit you are dealing with.

Distracting the dog as soon as it starts licking can work. First, interrupt the dog without directly rewarding the licking. For instance, offering a bone could be seen as a direct reward for licking, whereas walking to the kitchen or opening the back door is an effective distraction followed by asking for a sit, down or paw. Then give the bone. Stroking the dog while it is licking is a direct reward, whereas calling him to you and then stroking him or giving him a cuddle will more likely reward him for coming when called (1.5 - and 1.13).

Using 'leave it' training can be invaluable with this – but the dog needs to know the command well (10.12) and be responding reliably without treats.

Raising the dog's pleasure levels by feeding them differently (1.17) and providing an interesting selection of toys which are rotated to keep interest, can provide useful distractions. Telling the dog 'No!' whenever it begins to lick should get the point across but beware – it can result in 'secret licking'. A substance called 'No Lick' is available from most veterinary surgeons. These foul-tasting droplets, placed around the licked area, will make your dog think twice about 'tucking in'.

Luca, a Cavapoo, started licking his leg in the evenings to get his owners attention if they had not taken him into work that day. He was checked out by the vet as he had ongoing skin problems – but his leg was given a clean bill of health. Just feeding him differently and introducing trick training coupled with 'leave it' stopped the licking.

If the dog is not hurting itself, causing bald patches or licking disproportionately, you need do nothing. Regular grooming is normal.

8.09 Tail Chasing

This behaviour is usually born out of boredom, stress or frustration – the repeated action makes the dog feel better, rather like pacing up and down the living room. Your reaction to the tail chasing can quickly turn it into an attention-seeking game.

Deal directly with the boredom or frustration by giving the dog more fun and mental stimulation (1.7, 1.17 and Chapter 10). Tail chasing can be a hard habit to break – there is so much enjoyment to be had by doing it. Removing the fun from the pursuit possibly by employing time-outs (1.11) may be the only way to completely stop it occurring.

Monty, a very lively Jack Russell Terrier, was on limited exercise due to an injury. He began attacking his tail during his recuperation because he was bored. Monty would suddenly spy his tail like it was a lurking trespasser sneaking up on him, and start attacking it, growling and spinning as he did so. Giving Monty fun things to do that didn't involve him moving around too much took away the need to chase his tail and avoided further injury and a bad habit.

8.10 Shadow and Light Chasing

Becoming mildly attracted to a shadow or reflection flickering on the wall (from a metal watch strap for instance) is totally normal for most dogs. The sudden movement catches their attention. It can be a nice way for them to entertain themselves. Occasionally, a dog will become too engrossed in this occupation, and may try to jump at or pounce on the shadow or light beam, knocking ornaments flying or causing damage to walls. This is pure sport to a dog that doesn't think about the carnage he's causing.

If a dog has only just started doing this he can often be stopped by an abrupt time-out or two (1.11 and 1.14) offset by other gratifying things to do throughout the day, removing the need to chase lights and shadows. A swift 'leave it' command could be all you need with a dog that has learned this well (10.12), but this can take many months to train for and with time being of the essence to avoid a habit forming perhaps consider something else.

If he's already acquired a bad habit remove the element of

entertainment using the suggestions in 1.10, 1.12 and 1.14. As with all such problems, the dog must be stopped in the midst of behaving badly, and not told off minutes or hours later (1.13). When you leave the house, the safest way to avoid damage is to keep the dog out of the room in which he chases shadows.

Henry, an enthusiastic light-chasing English Springer Spaniel, had stripped off large sections of wallpaper in his excitement at chasing the beams of light radiating off a wind chime by the back door. Removing the chimes stopped the problem for a while, until Henry discovered moving shadows in the living room, which came through the patio door and were cast by the trees and shrubs in the garden. Unwilling to uproot foliage to foil his dog, Henry's owner decided to deal directly with his pooch's irritating hobby. Using a water-squirter, Henry got a verbal warning (I think he used 'don't you dare') followed by a well-aimed shot in the chops as soon as he looked at the shadows and his tail started wiggling in anticipation. This worked exceptionally and he quickly gave up the pursuit on hearing just the warning. Henry was not left alone very often, and his owner closed the curtains when he did have to go out, which stopped any repeat performances happening in his absence.

8.11 Insect Obsessions

Watching a dog diving in the garden after a butterfly is quite entertaining and harmless. Most dog's reactions are not quick enough to catch insects. As with shadow and light chasers above, this sport is normal for a dog and can provide endless hours of outdoor fun in the summer but can cause broken ornaments if pursued at length in the house. Scooting after a spider scampering across the living room floor might be fun for the dog, but it can send an arachnophobe owner (like me) into a blind panic. Why dogs always have to play with the spider under my nose defeats me! Chasing bees and wasps in the same way is a cause for concern as a dog could easily be stung. You would think this would cure him of the habit, but a sting could endanger his health or even his life. Following the advice given in the section above should help if this activity starts to cause problems. As with all annoying 'doggy sports', the quicker you tackle the issue the easier it is to stop.

CHAPTER NINE

Reactive / Aggressive Dogs

9.1 *Moods*

Moods govern behaviour; the way we feel can affect how we react to what is going on around us. If we are feeling happy generally, we can cope well with all types of situations. On the other hand, if we are feeling low, then anything that happens can make us feel even lower – even if it is something nice.

Reactive is a rebranding of the term aggressive and is popularly seen as a more palatable description for the everyday dog owner.

Aggression is in us all. It is a survival strategy we use when we are very frightened. It helps us to defend ourselves. When someone makes you suddenly jump out of your skin, you either giggle and laugh it off or, if they have really scared you, your self-defence system kicks in and you are ready to fight for your life! Aggression is usually only resorted to when there is no other option available. Contrary to popular opinion, aggression or being reactive is not all about physical attacks. Most species of animals across the globe use aggression as a means of potentially avoiding conflict. For instance, in humans the louder you shout and scream, the more likely it is your opponent will back down or runaway – thus avoiding harm. Other species use what they have – flapping wings, changing colour – you get the idea. These are termed aggressive displays and are widely used as a form of defence from monkeys to birds to bears to fish…

Getting angry is not just about self-defence, it is also an emotional safety valve, something we all use at some point in our lives to stop us breaking down. When you explode you feel quite good, as this is nature's way of relieving your intense frustration, bringing you back to normal. Only when you look around, and your family peer out from behind the furniture, does remorse kick in.

People and animals rarely get aggressive without a strong and disturbing reason (the exception to this is brain disorders or severe mental illness, where the person or animal has no emotional control). With dogs, their situation is rarely life-threatening, but they don't necessarily know that, and the many triggers that can spark an aggressive episode are usually highly emotional and unique to the individual.

9.2 Fear

Being really afraid is a horrible feeling, especially if you cannot escape what is frightening you (8.1 – 8.3). Not being able to get away increases the likelihood of becoming reactive. Many dogs are aggressive because they are very afraid. And having used the strategy once, they are more likely to use it again – because it works. A dog that is frightened of someone approaching may begin to bark and lunge forward, with hackles up and bared teeth. There are not many people who could ignore this, and most of us would walk away or at least back up a little. Even if that person didn't go away, we would take our loutish dog off as quickly as we could. Instant success for the dog – and that episode is filed away as a good method of getting rid of something scary.

A dog that may have been terrified by other people now becomes highly reactive in any threatening situation. It can appear quite confident – because it has learned exactly how to deal with the threat. A wagging tail is a good indicator of how happy the dog feels using aggression. The front end may be ugly and loud while the back-end wags energetically (always go by what the front end is doing!).

Ignoring this problem will not make it go away. The dog feels rewarded by being aggressive and getting a reaction from its target often increases the aggression – and the reward! For example, let's say a dog walking down the street on a lead with its owner spies another dog. It goes stiff momentarily (this is when it starts to feel rewarded or get a thrill), then begins barking, lunging and maybe spinning on the lead. If the other dog ignores it, the aggressive dog will calm down soon after its target has gone out of sight. If the target dog begins to bark back, then the whole game is raised to another level, and it can take many minutes for the dog to return to normal. What a buzz! The poor owner, hanging onto the lead for dear life, can do nothing but wait. Pulling back on the lead only increases the dog's urge to pull forward (think about if you want to get to something or someone. If you are pulled back or restrained, the emotional intensity of your desire is greatly increased). Shouting at the dog will often increase the passion, as it tends to fuel aggression – think of warriors in battle – and maybe the dog will believe you are joining in too!

9.3 Reactive to Dogs and People

Taking the fun out of the aggression or making it fail is the sensible way forward. To be effective, you have to do this at the precise moment when the dog starts to feel good about his reactive behaviour. Timing is crucial to ensure the dog does not enjoy any pleasurable feelings from being aggressive. First, try using your 'leave it' training (10.12) if your dog is proficient at it, or the 'enough' approach (3.14) if you use it at home followed by ignoring for thirty seconds.

If these do not reap rewards try using one of the stronger suggestions in 1.10 and 1.12 (with a reminder of timing in 1.13 and 1.14), just before or as soon as the dog begins to react, and this will often stop his hysterics in its tracks.

Jack, a medium-sized crossbreed, was very loud towards people and other dogs when out walking. He had not met many dogs or people when he was very young and found them very threatening. As a youngster he would pull back on the lead or hide behind his 'Mum'. One day Jack felt so threatened by another dog that was desperate to play, that he barked and showed his teeth until the playful dog ran off. Jack thus learned to be reactive to cope with frightening things, and he became a very difficult dog to walk.

Using a bleep/spray collar (1.10 and 1.12), the sport was taken out of his aggression, and Jack went back to being afraid and hiding behind his 'Mum'. The bleep was activated immediately Jack went stiff on seeing someone. The spray followed only when Jack did not heed the bleep warning. At this point, when he was no longer being loud and nasty, it was possible to introduce Jack slowly and carefully to calm and relaxed dogs and friendly, non-threatening people, to build up his confidence. A simple way of doing this was to praise and treat for every person or dog he walked past without reacting. It took nearly three months for Jack to begin to feel comfortable around others. It was crucial to break the habit of aggression and then address the underlying cause for Jack's behaviour problem, because if he'd started to feel threatened again, he would have gone back to his old reactive ways.

A Pet Corrector™ can be used to solve this type of problem, but the dog must be on a lead right by the owner's side and the can shown/phrase said immediately the dog begins to react. Using a walking aid such as a head collar or front-attaching harness is often very useful, as it helps to control a dog and reduce the lunging forward. It also enables the dog to be promptly turned and walked away to get him out of a threatening situation.

Each time a dog uses aggression, as Jack did, it reinforces the idea that it works – so he is likely to use it again.

9.4 On Lead Aggression

There are two main reasons why dogs are reactive when on a lead – frustration and fear. We all feel frustrated when we want something badly but can't have it. If a dog is very playful with other dogs off the lead, but barks and jumps about excitedly on the lead, it could be that he desperately wants to go and play or visit the other dog – but because he is held back, he becomes annoyed. A dog like this can be helped just by walking him out in the company of other dogs, which reduces the excitement he feels on seeing a dog across the street. Many dog walkers offer group walks.

As we saw in 9.2 above, fear can be all consuming. Being on the lead reduces options; you can't run away, so fighting may be the next best choice. Some dogs are attacked or pestered by other dogs while they are on the lead, so the situation becomes scary. The dog on the lead may shy away initially, but a forceful or particularly playful dog may not heed this and keep after them. So, the restrained dog has little choice but self-defence.

A rescued crossbreed, Brock, was brought to me because he was very agitated. When he saw other dogs on a walk he would spin on the lead and bark until he frothed at the mouth or bit his tongue. He had never been off the lead with his new owners because of his problem. At my behaviour clinic we did a doggy introduction, on the lead, to see exactly how he behaved. We used my colleague's very placid female Rottweiler as Brock's 'date'. Brock became so enraged he broke his lead and went hurtling across the room towards the Rottweiler, who stood totally still in a state of shock. When Brock got there, he wagged his tail, sniffed the other dog all over, and tried to get her to play with him. It took us a few seconds to recover from what had just happened, by which time everything was fine – all except for the Rottweiler – who was promptly sick!

Brock was an extremely reactive-looking animal on the lead, but off it he was playful and fun. By mixing him with other dogs off the lead in the local park, Brock's owners made doggy friends who they then walked out with, reducing Brock's problem dramatically. After this fraught experience we made it a rule at the clinic always to use two leads on the really aggressive-looking dogs. Then all we had to do was to sort out the poor Rottweiler.

The way we handle the lead can also cause problems of frustration or fear. Pulling back on the lead, shortening or tightening it when another person or dog is coming, can cause a dog to behave badly. Just by doing this we may make the dog think there is something scary coming – so beware! If the dog is excited at the prospect of meeting someone new, or an unknown dog, our tugging on the lead can turn this excitement into annoyance. Walking a dog on a relatively short lead in busy areas (so the lead is loose and the dog by your side but not on the other side of the pavement) takes away the need to rein the dog in. If the dog is on a long lead and there are people approaching – use the 'come here' signal, ask the dog to sit, and make a fuss of him while you shorten the lead. This turns the dog's perception of the situation into 'training' as opposed to 'threat'. Using a head collar or a front-attaching harness, instead of a back-attaching harness or normal neck collar, can help. Once a dog is used to wearing a head collar or harness, they are often calmer on the lead and don't choke as with the collar.

Nagging on the lead is a bad, human habit. I see people

doing it all the time, often for no reason, particularly with German Shepherd dogs. The dog is sitting minding its own business and the owner makes little jerking actions with the lead, yank, yank, yank. It irritates me so I dread to think how the dog feels. The dog then starts lunging and barking at all and sundry. This is one way that security firms gee dogs up to make them look aggressive, not something we want to encourage in our pets, so watch what you are doing with that lead!

9.5 The Cornered Dog

Animals become very reactive if they are frightened and then trapped – it is simple self-defence. Cornering a dog and then telling him off is not a good idea if you value your relationship with him. Titus was a Neapolitan Mastiff – a very, very big, grey dog! At around a year old he began to growl menacingly at his 'Dad' and occasionally at his 'Mum'. He then became suspicious of visitors and had to be shut out if anyone came to the house. In the days before I had my behaviour centre, I saw problem animals in the client's home. Titus was shut out in the garden when I arrived, so I sat down on the sofa. His 'Dad' fetched him in on the thickest choke chain I have ever seen and hung on for dear life as Titus headed in my direction. With both their feet slipping on the laminate floor, Titus succeeded in dragging his 'Dad' towards his target – me. So much for choke chains! With one last pull, 'Dad' managed to wrestle Titus out of the room and shut the door. Breathing a sigh of relief does not accurately sum up the situation – what I needed was a change of underwear!

Titus's first outburst of aggression had occurred when he was told off by his 'Dad'. This took the form of being chased into the garden and smacked. Titus had rolled onto his back and peed, spraying his enraged 'Dad' – who then vented his anger by shouting at him. By rolling on his back, Titus had basically said 'I'm sorry' in the strongest way he knew how. When his 'Dad' remained angry, Titus felt threatened and defended himself in the only way he could. He became angry. From then on, he became mistrustful of his owner, and other people, and used aggression to deal with any situation that bothered him – because it worked!

Getting Titus's trust back was the main emotional issue. Aggression was behaviour he had learned. A remote-controlled bleep/spray collar was used (1.10 and 1.12) when he got aggressive – it was vital Titus did not realise it was his owner 'telling him off'. Fun was the order of the day to rebuild the relationship between Titus and his 'Mum' and 'Dad'. Providing treats, increasing games and taking time-out just to stroke and cuddle Titus put the pleasure back into the situation from all sides. Removing the heavy choke chain and replacing it with a head collar allowed Titus to be walked more and gave his owners confidence they could hold him if he pulled. It also stopped them yanking him whenever a person or dog appeared on the walk. Titus was given a bleep if he growled at anyone and was ignored for thirty seconds, and a treat if he didn't. With this very clear signalling system, it didn't take Titus long to realise that aggression was no longer working for him, and that people were sources of pleasure rather than fear.

It was also important for the owners to understand why Titus had become reactive. We do need to tell dogs off occasionally, otherwise they can get out of control. But the punishment needs to be swift, while the dog is doing wrong, and should be over and done with quickly (see 1.13 and 1.14). Staying cross with them for minutes, hours or days serves no purpose other than to undermine your relationship. If you continue to punish them in your anger you can force them to defend themselves against you. A dog only needs to become aggressive once, and find aggression works for them, and they will apply this strategy regularly.

9.6 Reactive to Children

Children can be unpredictable in their behaviour, and so can our dogs. Put the two together and you have a potentially explosive situation. I was first bitten as an eighteen-month-old child. Sneaking through a gap in the fence to next-door's garden as my mother hung out the washing, I approached the retriever who lived there and stuck my fingers up his nostrils. He bit me in the face. My mother was there immediately, but it all happened very quickly – as these things do. As a five-year-old I snuck up behind Puffin, our almost blind Boston Terrier, who was stealing biscuits out of a bag on the floor. He was tense because he was thieving and he knew he shouldn't be, and as I prodded him on the bottom, he turned and bit me on the arm. My Dad told both me and Puffin off, as I should not have snuck up on him and he shouldn't have bitten me. These are typical daily hazards for dog owners with kids.

Most dogs are fond of children, and under parental supervision they make great mischief together. But when a dog is not used to children, he can find them quite scary. Children move quickly, can be very loud and have a tendency to stare at dogs at their own level, looking directly into the dog's eyes. Very young children can grab at a dog's tail, pull its ears, or do what I did and stick fingers in nose holes. Most dogs will not put up with this for long. If they can get away, they do. If they are cornered or have nowhere to escape the errant child, they might growl or snap.

We need to monitor our dogs when they're with young children, however much we trust them to be good. It only takes one second for a dog to bite a child, but the run-up to it is often obvious and avoidable. You can bond a child with a dog by teaching the child how to throw a toy for it or give it a treat. It's also important to tell a child off for being unpleasant to a dog, as you would if the child was about to put its fingers in an electrical socket. You shouldn't push your pet's tolerances to the limit where children are concerned, and you certainly don't want to wait until the dog decides to tell the child off itself!

Some dogs simply cannot cope with children. If a dog hasn't been taught how to behave around kids, and has had no experience of them, then we are expecting a lot for it to be happy and relaxed with children running around. This is an area where sometimes our expectations of dogs are unrealistic. If a dog is reactive to children, then it perhaps should be muzzled (9.7) and put on a lead in areas where children might be. Then following the guidance in 9.3 you can safely tackle the issue.

When a dog is aggressive to other dogs, I often use a calm, confident 'stooge' dog to show the aggressive dog that not all other dogs are scary, and some want to be friends. It is unethical to use children in the same context. A child that has been bitten or seriously frightened by a dog can be put off them for life – although that didn't apply to me.

9.7 Angry at the Vets

Given that most dogs only go to the vet once per year for a booster injection, most of them cope well. A dog that becomes reactive in the consultation room makes it almost impossible for the vet to check its health or treat it for illness. Trying to muzzle the angry animal once it has become aggressive carries a risk of getting bitten – and increases the stress the dog is under. Fussing and praising your dog to calm it down does exactly the opposite.

If you know your dog gets upset and angry in this situation, then get the dog used to wearing a muzzle at home. With a basket type you can smear tasty cream cheese or peanut butter into the muzzle and allow the dog to lick at it. Do this regularly, a few times per day. Once the dog is happy to place its face in the muzzle pop it on for a few minutes and post treats through the gaps Then put the muzzle on the dog for a few minutes each day, so it becomes a regular occurrence. Lots of fuss and attention should be given while the dog is wearing the muzzle, but when you take it off try not to cuddle the dog, as the relief of having it removed is reward enough. While getting them used to wearing a muzzle, also work on using a head collar to give you that extra bit of control when in the surgery. Use the same technique as with the muzzle but remember to clip on a lead and walk them out on it a few times.

If you put these on at home, head collar on first and muzzle over the top, before you get in the car and drive to the vet, you will avoid the problem of trying to truss the dog up once you are there. This also reduces the stress factor for the dog. A dog that can't bite allows a vet to do his job properly and effectively – and that's what you are paying them for! By making sure the dog's aggression strategy doesn't work, you help him become resigned to his examination.

Many dogs cause fewer problems at the vets if their owners leave them there or the vet takes the dog into another room away from its owners. This is always worth a try if a dog is being difficult, and the veterinary practice is agreeable. Getting the vet to make friends with your dog and give him treats can work in some situations, but when a dog is truly upset by the whole vet experience, he may take the treats and bite the vet anyway!

It is always better to be proactive where trips to the vets are concerned. You know your dog needs to go at least once per year, perhaps more if it is poorly. Pop your dog in weekly, then monthly for weigh-ins and fuss from the nurses. Make life easy for yourself and do this right from the start, not once you have a problem – by then you have a huge mountain to climb.

9.8 Reactive to Other Animals

Fear or uncertainty is usually the underlying cause of a dog being aggressive to animals such as horses or cows. The most obvious solution is to keep the dog away from areas where the animals are. A dog that is battering the rabbit hutch needs to have a fence erected so it cannot get to it, or the rabbit should be moved to a safer location. If it is not possible to keep the dog away, then applying some of the techniques in 9.3 may help to take the sport out of their aggression.

Tommy, a young Collie, made a beeline for the bird cage every time he managed to sneak through into the living room. He frightened Eddison, the parrot, by jumping up and yapping, and Eddison then squawked and puffed himself up in response. This intense reaction spurred Tommy on, and he then had to be manhandled out of the room and the situation was avoided again for many weeks. As we didn't want to upset Eddison by using anything noisy and with the problem being specific to the house the obvious solution was time-outs (1.10, 1.11 and 1.14), coupled with lots of repetition rather than a one-off trip to the room occasionally. Being a Collie, Tommy was quick to learn and soon became deferential to Eddison and was allowed to enjoy the benefits of the living room, including the rug by the fire and Eddison swiftly learned to bark!

Some dogs are natural hunters, while others are not. This doesn't always depend on the breed – it's more an individual, personality thing. If you have a dog that chases cats and squirrels and goes crazy when a hedgehog is in the garden, you must assume it will follow through with the pounce/bite/

kill part of the dog's natural hunting sequence. It is prudent to be careful where this type of dog is allowed off-lead. Pet correctors™ and bleep/spray devices tend not to work for hunters, as their response is often not purely emotional but instinctive and is governed by a different part of the brain. If you have a real hunter – accept it. Manage potential problems by keeping the dog on lead in areas where there is wildlife and muzzling it when off lead.

9.9 Grooming Difficulties

One stroke of the brush, one piece of cheese. Dogs can be a little tetchy about being touched or groomed. They can cope well with their back and chest being brushed but venturing towards the rear end or feet can turn the animal into a snarling frenzy. The main cause of this is knots (or cots as they say in Leicester). Getting a snag caught in a sensitive area can be painful to a dog. The dog will often allow you to touch the area with your hand, but if you have a brush in it – beware! Have you ever been snipped on the ear by a hairdresser, or poked a little too harshly by a dental hygienist? It makes you feel very vulnerable, and a little defensive. The trust between you and your hygienist has to be very strong for you to continue to allow them to poke around between your teeth. This is no different from how a dog might feel upon having a knot brushed out in one swift and sweeping movement. Pain is very individual. Some can take it quite well (and perhaps enjoy it). Others crumble physically and emotionally at the slightest twinge.

Regaining trust and confidence can take time. Give one gentle sweep of the brush, reward the dog with one sliver of cheese, and limit each session to a few minutes or a few strokes. It can be helpful to have two pairs of hands in the early stages – one to administer the food, while the other wields the brush. Hannah, my German Shepherd, had very bad hips, and the pain of being brushed was obviously very unpleasant for her in those areas. My husband would lie on the floor feeding her nice bits and pieces while I quickly groomed her back legs and tail. She tolerated the intrusion on her painful areas, as long as the food was still coming thick and fast.

For the real biters, a muzzle is the only safe solution (9.7). Muzzling takes away the option of biting and gives you confidence to get on with the job in hand. You do need to be careful, though, not to hurt the dog further, which would totally convince him that grooming isn't nice. Sending a dog to the grooming parlour can be a good decision. Many dogs are fine when it's not their owner wielding the brush. They may cope better when groomed in a different place by a new person. Do make the groomer aware of any potential hazards.

It is also important to consider the type of brush you are wielding. Some are quite harsh and need to be used carefully so as not to hurt the dog's skin.

9.10 Temper Tantrums

Like a thrashing two-year-old in a supermarket, some of our dogs can have temper tantrums – usually if things aren't going quite their way. These outbursts have teeth! Dogs like this are not common but if you have one then when you ask him to get off the sofa, don't be surprised if he acts all grumpy and growls. He is comfortable where he is and the prospect of having to move may make him cross. These particular dogs have a hard time coping with frustration or disappointment. We have to look at these situations very carefully and analyse the dog's general emotional state. If a dog is generally very happy, losing a treat is insignificant. If it is generally unhappy, the loss of a luxury becomes a major international incident!

Dogs that are unable to cope with the feelings of disappointment, or the prospect of a reward being taken away, can react with an immediate and highly charged response of frustration and rage. These dogs usually have very little that is rewarding in their lives, and so they value the rewards they get above all else. They could be described as Dr Jekyll and Mr Hyde characters, usually over-affectionate with frequent moody spells. They may spend many hours in their beds, grumbling or signalling in some way that they 'want to be alone'.

One compensation with this type of aggressive dog is that it is unlikely that a stranger will be bitten. That pleasure is usually reserved for close family members. Such dogs tend to fall into two categories – the dog that has suddenly become reactive, and the dog that has been like it from puppyhood.

9.11 Grumpy Dogs

A dog doesn't just suddenly wake up with a different character. It changes imperceptibly over the weeks or months until you suddenly notice that your normally happy dog is sullen and grumpy. In my experience there are many things that cause this. Divorce or any sudden change in the dog's personal circumstances, which may mean he now spends long periods of time on his own. Another example is prolonged illness – where the animal has been confined to a crate or on-lead exercise and has had very little fun. Being rehoused, perhaps several times, can also be very unsettling to a dog and can cause it to feel very unhappy. Being in constant (even low grade) discomfort, like with arthritis or a sore back is a common presenter and being over tired perhaps caused by an owner retiring from work or suddenly working from home.

These starting points all have one common element -

they involve some sort of upset to the dog. It could be that there is not one big upset, but several small ones. In many cases the dogs are fine for the majority of the time but have grumpy periods, often when they are tired or hungry. Most owners report seeing a sudden change overcome their pet; a stiffening of the body and a strange darkening or hardening of the eyes, turning them into 'devil's eyes'. The rage is sudden and severe, and unless the poor owner is well prepared, often ends up in a nasty bite (these bites tend not to be the nip and retreat of a frightened animal, but a sustained attack). Living with a dog like this is heart-breaking – as they are so loyal and affectionate most of the time – and you never quite know when the next explosion will come.

Making the dog feel better is the first priority – dealing with his underlying emotional and or physical state. A trip to the vets for a thorough check-up is essential for this. Many dogs with this problem are stiff and sore but as it comes on gradually the owner doesn't see it. Only then can we begin to address the specific situations that the dog reacts to – the learned or habitual behaviour. A simple way to make a dog feel better is to offer more of what he likes. Increased exercise and fun games, getting new toys, and feeding him differently are ideas that are easy to implement (1.5 - 1.7 and 1.17). There are many natural calmers on the market that can help lift a dog's mood. If a dog is feeling very low it may not want to play or run around, and an internal as well as an external boost can help.

Ensuring the dog is well rested is also crucial. Dogs like sleep and need lots of it, much more than us and preferably without continual interruptions. The common theme is owners who work from home or are at home a lot of the time. Every time they move, the dog moves and never really gets enough sleep. This is where a crate or special area for the dog comes into its own, a place where the dog can rest for a few hours each day without us continually waking it up. One of the signs where this is a possibility is the dog that does not wake readily in the morning and is grumpier in the late afternoon/evening.

I have had many aggression cases where just offering proper sleep has stopped the aggression completely. I have also had many cases of this type that have responded well to anti-inflammatories/pain relief from their vet coupled with physiotherapy. Try to consider all the factors from the dog's point of view.

9.12 The Spoilt Brat

Just as you can spoil a child, you can also spoil a dog. Not, as you might imagine, by giving it lots of attention, treats, toys and walks – this is what our pets should be getting anyway. But if you never say no to him, your dog will never learn to control his emotions in that situation. Giving in to their demands all the time turns both our children and our dogs into brats! These dogs are likely to have a turn in any situation where they need correcting. If they're spoilt, they're likely to be stroppy and prone to tantrums all their lives.

Spoilt dogs need to be taught to cope with frustration and disappointment very gradually. To make sudden changes at home and expect a dog to welcome them is naive. Food-dispensing toys are a great way to help a dog with this problem (1.17). When they nudge the toy, they want the contents but are not too sure how to get them. So, they nudge harder, and a few pieces of food drop out. They push again, and when nothing happens, they push harder... all of which teaches them to cope with frustration without getting cross. Clicker training is another way to help a dog cope with disappointment – teaching him to try harder instead of getting upset (1.5 – 1.7). The basic principle we need to get across to the dog is that the rewards are still there, they just have to control themselves a bit better to get them. This is no different from a parent walking away from a screaming child in a shop. There is no reward in that behaviour – try something else!

Reverse time-outs can be invaluable (1.11 but adapt it). With a typical time-out we are putting the dog in a place he doesn't want to be (garden in the cold, downstairs toilet, porch) but just for two minutes. Then we allow him back in as though nothing has happened. This is all done calmly, with no shouting or emotion. With reverse time-outs the humans leave the room, calmly and quietly, which is a safer option when dealing with an angry mutt. The upshot is the same. The dog is isolated from the family for a few minutes as a result of behaving badly. The typical reaction to this is that the dog is standing by the door wagging its tail when everyone comes back in. Don't be tempted to greet it, ignore it for thirty seconds (1.15) and then carry on as though nothing has happened. This is crucial - any attention on re-entering the room can reward the punishment and give mixed messages (1.14).

Using the bleep/spray collar as in 1.10 and 1.12 can be very beneficial in breaking the aggressive cycle in these cases as the dog can be unaware the owner is operating it.

9.13 Grumpy in Bed

A dog that grumbles in his bed could be feeling threatened. If we make their bed a place of punishment, they may feel that they're being punished as long as they stay there. Anyone approaching the bed could be seen as a direct threat, since the dog anticipates further punishment. Or the dog could be feeling emotionally low, or most commonly, just tired (we're all more susceptible to grumpiness when tired). The dog may well have gone to bed, his sanctuary, to get away from the family, because he needed some peaceful sleep – only to have his peace disturbed, which causes him to growl. If, as a result of his growling, the dog is left alone he will feel his aggression has succeeded and growl the next time this happens.

There is a lot of sense in the old adage 'let sleeping dogs lie'. Dogs don't go to their bed to be tidy – they are often tired or want to chill out for a while. Disturbing a dog in its bed should only be for a reason that benefits the dog!

We should try to make the dog feel happy about us being near his bed. To keep going up to him, and then tell him off for growling, only makes the dog feel more threatened and upset. Try dropping surprise treats into the bed as you walk past, which will make a dog anticipate your approach with eagerness. Don't make a big thing of it – just drop the treat by their heads as you sail on by.

You could make it a rule that if the dog is in his bed, he should be left totally alone, this will help him to relax there. By 'left alone' I mean no eye contact, no talking to him or about him, and certainly no touching! The dog should be treated as if he was invisible in his bed, and you don't want to draw any attention to him. A printed sign above his bed could visually remind family members to follow this.

I've had at least one dog in my bed since I was a toddler so for me it's perfectly normal to have a 'sleep heap' at night where we all cuddle up. Some dogs can't cope with this and lash out in the night possibly because we are snoring and keeping them awake, thrashing around in the throes of a nightmare or getting up frequently to the loo. This is a particularly vulnerable time for us and it's not easy to deal with an angry dog when you're half asleep. Maybe it is better for all that these individuals have their own sleeping place where they can snooze away peacefully and get a goodnights rest.

9.14 *Tetchy on the Furniture*

Most dogs are happy to get off the furniture when asked. They have no bad feelings about it and do it willingly. When a dog doesn't, and has a growl or a snap, this means he is unhappy about getting off. We have to ask ourselves whether the dog is generally grumpy, or just grumpy about this. We have to make the dog feel happy about giving up his 'treat'. The easiest way to do this is to compensate him for his loss.

Using a treat tin that rattles, or the rustle of a treat packet in another room, call the dog. Give him a treat for coming. Over several days do this nearer and nearer to the sofa (try not to overdo it as the dog may get irritated). Change what you say to the dog. Instead of 'come here', maybe use 'off you get'. Keep your voice soft and happy to lift the dog's mood. As with coming when called, (10.8), we need to cut down the number of treats given – so the dog is never sure when a treat is on offer or not. Toys, particularly squeaky ones, can be very helpful in stimulating the dog's interest. Squeak the toy and start to play with it. Use your 'off you get' signal at the same time. When the dog comes to you, play with him for a few minutes. Dogs that learn this way will often get off the sofa and go like a heat-seeking missile for the nearest toy to play with. Working on the problem in this way and considering the dog's feelings at giving up his seat, means you can still allow him on the furniture when you want to.

Another option is to stop the dog getting up there in the first place and offer him a nice comfortable duvet bed in the living room instead. You may have to share the sofa with the vacuum cleaner for a while, so you can block all access to the furniture while the dog is learning. Putting the duvet bed at the other end of the room may make it too far away from you to interest the dog. Place the bed as near to you as possible. A fluffy blanket for the dog to scuff up and a tasty chewy bone can be added to make him feel it is his special place.

9.15 Toy and Food Guarding

Dogs are often taught to do this by having toys pulled out of their mouths and their food taken away from them. A dog isn't born to defend a ball, it learns to defend it, and if you don't threaten the dog's food, it won't have to protect it. By looking at the problem from the dog's emotional point of view, you can see that his guarding comes from feeling threatened. The dog simply can't cope with the thought of losing his toy or his food, and the feelings of disappointment can be overwhelming.

9.16 Dealing with Food Guarding

It is often the food bowl that the dog is guarding. To find out if this is the case, try feeding the dog from a food toy or on a plate. If the dog begins to guard these then place an empty food bowl or plate onto the floor. Have the food measured out into a bowl in the kitchen. Place one small handful of food in the bowl and wait for the dog to eat it. Then place the next handful of food in the bowl. Continue like this until all the food is eaten. This removes the feeling of threat, as you are actually giving the dog each bit of dinner and not taking any away. This exercise, which can take many weeks, needs to be followed until the dog is relaxed and happy with you near his food bowl.

Feeding the dog all of his food as treats through training can restore his confidence in you as a 'parent'. You become the major source of rewards, which includes giving him his dinner bit by bit throughout the day.

Another tried and tested method is to give him 'pudding'. Have your mobile on you or something to distract yourself with. When preparing the dogs dinner on the kitchen worktop put a separate plate beside it. Go into the treat cupboard and retrieve a couple of delicious goodies (the 'pudding') and pop them on the plate. Make sure he sees all of this. Place his dinner on the floor and turn away so you are not looking at him. Read your phone to stop you staring at him. Do not move away. Once he has finished his dinner put the 'pudding' down and again turn away and scour your mobile. When the greedy mutt has relaxed over his dinner, a few days or weeks perhaps, you can stop turning away - eventually, maybe months later you may actually engage with him. I love this method as it encourages your dog to want you to remain present while he's eating.

9.17 The Chocolate Factory Method

I don't know if it's true, but rumour has it if you work for a chocolate factory you can eat as much of the brown stuff as you like. The theory goes that very quickly the desire to consume dissipates rapidly – reducing theft and the like.

For very serious food-guarding issues, where the dog is obsessive about his bowl and does not respond to being fed bit by bit, try feeding ad lib. Fill up the food bowl, leave it down all the time, and top it up as and when required. This suggestion should only be followed when all else has been tried and failed.

The dog will gorge himself horribly for the first few days. There may be messes in the house, particularly overnight, as the dog's eating pattern has significantly altered. There is the risk of tummy trouble through over-eating, which can be serious. It is not advisable to use a dry food that expands in the dog's stomach (moisten a piece of food with water and wait to see if it gets much bigger – if it does, change the diet), as this can make the tummy swell to dangerous proportions. Needless to say, you should be around for the first few days to keep a close eye on the dog's health. His general mood may also be affected, as he no longer has the anticipation of food as a treat, so games and fun activities should be increased.

Ad lib feeding may make a food-obsessed dog more stressed to start with. You can reduce this stress by using a plug-in diffuser that releases happy doggy smells into the air, or a mood-lifting dietary supplement (or both!) to help him cope better.

Dobby, a Collie cross, came to live with me when he was seven months old. He was on a one-way visit to the vet as he was biting over food and growling when approached or in his bed. Using many of the above techniques we managed to make him feel happy about his bed and controlled his food aggression by being very careful not to leave any food around. We also fed him slightly away from the other three dogs. Through training we taught him to sit and stay after he had finished his meal (which was inhaled rather than eaten), to stop him from stealing the others' food. Three months later, we were still in the same position – using safeguards and keeping a close eye on him around food. It became apparent we were only controlling the situation, not sorting it!

I had a few days off work so I could keep an eye on the dogs. I filled all four (very large) bowls up to the top with food and sat back to watch the party. All four dogs stuffed themselves to the hilt, and when they had finished, they waddled to a place in the kitchen and lay down. To their horror, I then filled all the bowls up again. Dobby and Tosca creaked and groaned as they made it back to the food and slowly began to eat a bit more. Bigun and Mutley admitted defeat graciously and fell asleep. All four dogs slept soundly that night and I set my alarm clock to get them out earlier than normal for their walk.

The next day all four dogs grazed on the food throughout the morning – the big rush was over. But at lunchtime Dobby became disturbed about the food bowls and began trying to empty them, picking food out and hiding it behind them.

His body language was hunched, his tail was tucked right underneath him, and he was growling. So, I opened the back door, went outside, and started to kick a football around. All the dogs followed and joined in with a great game. When we finally went back inside Dobby was normal again and he never repeated the burying behaviour.

The dogs went on to share bowls, and Dobby actually chewed his food – which helped his digestion and teeth. His food obsessive behaviour disappeared completely. We took food he stole off him without any grumpiness, and his constant search for grub was reduced to what I considered normal levels for a typically stomach-driven pup.

9.18 Dealing with Toy Guarding

'Swapsies' is the name of the game here. As with furniture and food issues, you need to make the dog feel happy sharing things. Teaching them to play fetch using two toys (10.14) can also help, as you immediately throw one toy once you have the other in your hand. Teaching a dog to leave, and be happy about it, requires good value rewards, patience and a happy attitude towards the dog so he doesn't feel threatened. For more information on teaching your dog to leave see 10.12.

9.19 Protecting Puppies

Another, more specific, cause of extreme sudden anger is hormonally influenced aggression. This occurs when a mother has young to feed and protect or is suffering from a false or phantom pregnancy. It is caused by a surge of progesterone, which comes after ovulation in readiness for pregnancy and the protection of a litter. Toys or owners' possessions often take the place of real puppies in a false pregnancy, with bitches often attempting to suckle and refusing to leave them even for basic functions such as toileting and feeding. When a mother has real pups to care for, aggression can be triggered if too many people or other animals are nearby. Certainly, for the first two to three weeks the mother needs a degree of privacy so she can care for her pups without feeling threatened. Housing them in an area of the house that is not a through route for everyone is a sensible option. Once the pups are past three weeks old the mother does not stay with them all of the time, and the possibility lessens of her becoming reactive if people approach.

Regardless of whether the puppies are real or not, the sensible solution is to ensure the mother feels secure, is not disturbed unnecessarily, and that strangers and visitors are kept to a minimum and away from the 'whelping' site. By playing along with a false pregnancy we allow the 'mother' the space and time to rear her 'pup' until she feels able to share it with the rest of the family.

If proper concern is shown for the protective mother, her normal temperament should return once the hormones have run their course. Ovario-hysterectomy (spaying or neutering) is the only permanent cure for repeated false pregnancies, but this cannot be undertaken until hormone levels have restored which often means the aggressive episode has passed. There is a high risk of further false pregnancies so neutering should be strongly considered.

9.20 Dogs Fighting at Home

Boys can have a tiff, and a day later be drinking in the pub together as though nothing has happened. Girls fall out, and World War III has begun. This is how it tends to be with us, and many of our dogs are no different. Dogs can have disagreements over many things, a toy, a bone or chew or jealousy over an owner's attention for example. When these disagreements are big, the love and bond between them can turn to hate, and our dogs become angry at the mere sight of each other. The fights that ensue are often terrifying and blood is spilt. In these situations, the relationship between the dogs breaks down so quickly it can sometimes be impossible to repair.

Cindy and Ellie were two young Yorkshire Terrier females. Ellie was very nervous of people while Cindy was a 'tart' who loved everyone. They were very different characters and got along famously, until Ellie had a season. Ellie picked a fight with Cindy, and being Terriers, it was a nasty one. Cindy then became afraid of Ellie and growled at her on sight. Ellie could not tolerate being growled at, so she attacked Cindy again and again. There is only one thing to do in this scenario, and that is to separate the dogs completely. Each time they meet and fight, the relationship deteriorates further. Cindy went to stay with family for a few weeks and Ellie remained at home. Once Ellie's season had finished both dogs were reintroduced to each other away from the house. They got on reasonably well, although Cindy was still very suspicious of Ellie. These suspicions were not unfounded, as Ellie attacked Cindy again when the owners tried to walk them back into the house. So, Cindy went back off to Grandma's. Frequent meetings over a six-week period, involving walks together and meeting up in the local park, rejuvenated their relationship, and both dogs became excited and happy on seeing one another. At this point Cindy moved back into the family home and the pair have been the best of friends ever since. Both dogs were neutered to avoid any hormonal trouble happening again. But hormones were just the trigger; it is very important to establish what caused the initial fight, and stop it happening again. Common factors are both dogs wanting the same toy, treat, meal, owner, at the same time. Simple jealousy. Once fighting had started, their relationship had to be built up from scratch. Using a natural calmer in their food and a plug-in 'happy smells' diffuser to keep the dogs as calm and peaceful as possible is also helpful. Identifying any particular chew or toy that sets the dogs off and sticking it in the bin is a must. Feeding the dogs in separate rooms is a must if that's where the battle lines are drawn. The quid pro quo technique in 1.16 is really useful to regain all round respect.

Of course, it is not always possible for a dog to stay with friends or relatives for the long periods needed for the healing process, and besides it doesn't always work – the bigger the love, the stronger the hate. Keeping dogs separated in the house can have the same effect, as long as they can tolerate each other outside on walks. If they can't, then one dog needs to be rehoused, a heart-wrenching decision to make but ultimately to the good of all.

A properly introduced water squirter or Pet Corrector™ (1.10 – 1.15) can be very effective in the early stages of this situation reinforcing the need to tackle problems as they surface rather than putting them off or excusing them.

9.21 Reactive in the Car

Once behind a glass window, a dog can become aggressive in the car – even to his owners. This can be because he feels he is now on guard duty and protecting your possessions against all comers, including you! A dog can also act aggressively because he's in a confined space and feels threatened through the window – someone passing may have teased him. A correctly introduced bleep/spray collar (1.12) can quickly sort out this problem (it will work through glass), allowing you to walk past your car window while teaching your dog that reactive behaviour will get him nowhere. Moving the dog to a different area of the car can also help.

Tamsin, a Cocker Spaniel, became reactive in the boot of

the car. She would lash out at her owner the instant she got in, making it very difficult for her to shut the boot door without being nipped. We put Tamsin in a car harness and offered her a place on the back seat of the car. Tamsin was happy with this arrangement and allowed herself to be strapped in. It was being in the boot that upset and frightened Tamsin; the back seat felt safer and was infinitely more comfortable!

CHAPTER TEN

Basic Training

10.1 How to Practise

I love dog training and taking classes – it is an absolute passion of mine. Seeing the light dawn in both species eyes as tasks start to come together is quite something to witness. And the relationship flourishes, as training a dog is all about opening up lines of communication between owner and dog. Learning to speak a bit of 'dog' if you like as he learns a morsel of 'human'!

One simple rule to follow is, *if he doesn't do, he doesn't get.* If you treat a dog for not doing something, just because you love him and he looks dead cute, then he will learn really quickly that he needn't bother – the treat will come anyway. Dogs are smart like that.

Training should be fun. A game. And it is excellent for mental stimulation (and for tiring out energetic dogs that can't be walked for long periods as they are still growing or injured). The trick with training is not to be too regimental about it. It's easy for a dog to do a task if you are standing there in front of it, clicker at the ready, treats bulging out of your hand. They get the idea that you want them to do something. It's harder to get a dog just to respond to you whenever you need it to – so that's what we need to practise.

What I find works is doing a short training session, perhaps five minutes twice per day, to specifically work on new things. Then, start adding your training techniques into normal life. Having your treats tucked into a pocket perhaps ask your dog to sit and stay in the kitchen while you put the kettle on. Go back, reward him, then ask him to stay again while you put tea bags into the pot. Again, go back and reward and maybe ask him to lie down. Tell him to stay while you pour the water and so on.

Once you get onto tasks such as 'out of sight stay', perhaps use a similar technique. Instead of letting your dog just follow you into the kitchen while you grab a drink (a beer would be good!), tell him to stay. You may need to step out of the room and immediately go back in and work your way up the hall with frequent trips back, but he's learning to do an out of sight stay in a normal setting, not a training session. And you are earning your beer.

When all is said and done, you need your dog to listen and respond in a normal family situation, so that's how I would recommend you practise. It makes it more fun as well and not a chore to train the dog, and you don't need to set aside any time to do it – so the age-old excuse of 'I haven't had time' just won't wash!

10.2 How to Use a Clicker

You do not have to use a clicker to train a dog. Saying 'good boy' followed by a treat can be just as good, so where you see 'click' in this Chapter, read 'good dog'. But for those of you who want to try this method – here we go.

A clicker is a small hand-held device that makes a 'click' sound when pressed. We use it for training dogs as a marker, to tell the dog he has done something right. Basically, click means tick! You've done something correctly. A treat or reward of some kind always follows the click, effectively telling the dog he's done it right AND a treat is coming. It makes training new tasks very quick and easy as the dog knows instantly when he has done something right and, more importantly, what he has done right. It makes it easy to get the dog then to repeat it. It is the immediacy and consistency of the click that makes it so effective.

Introducing a clicker couldn't be easier. Take a command which the dog knows already – typically sit. Ask him to sit, click as he sits and then give the food reward. Repeat this four or five times and he'll have got it.

A clicker is a training aid – it helps dogs to learn quickly. It is not one click for yes and two clicks for no. It is a simple click as the dog performs a task correctly, followed by a reward. Once the dog has achieved the task and is performing reliably, then you don't need to use the clicker (I know this is a concern of many people that if they use a clicker, they will always have to use it). If he gets lazy with any task, have a quick refresher using the clicker. You shouldn't be using the clicker for a sit when the dog is ten years old!

10.3 Name

Teaching a puppy or rescue dog its name is first in a long line of things they need to learn, and choosing the name is the first step. Two-syllable names are the easiest for our pets to grasp – for example Tosca, Mutley, Parsnip and Cricket. Long names are nice but may need shortening for everyday use.

Most dogs learn their names quickly without us really having to do any specific training for it. Just using it while paying a dog attention is often enough. If not, try this. Call your dog's name in a cheerful and excited voice, while it is quite close to you. If it looks around or comes to you, show you are happy by stroking it, giving it a food treat or offering a game of something it likes. Try not to over-use the name, as he may learn to ignore it. Only call him if you want him for something nice. Being called and then told off is a very quick method of teaching your dog its name is not a pleasant thing to hear.

10.4 Sit

A quick method to teach a young puppy to sit is to hold the food bowl over his head at dinnertime and wait. As soon as he sits down (often in frustration) say 'sit' and give him his dinner.

You can also teach this using a food treat. This method is a bit more versatile and not restricted to feeding time. Hold the treat over the pup's head, taking it just over the eye line very slowly. As the pup looks up and the treat starts to disappear over his head, he sits. There is no need to push down on the back end at all and in fact forcibly making a dog sit can make the whole process take longer as the dog instinctively pushes back.

You say 'sit' as the dog sits. Try saying it just the once as repeating it could make the signal 'sit sit sit' and the dog does not understand to respond to just 'sit'. The hand with the treat in is also serving as a hand signal and a dog will learn this visual signal faster than the word (a combination of hand signals and words is always the fastest way to get reliability). The hand signal I always stick to is just as if I have a treat in my hand and am holding it out in front of the pup (my thumb, first finger and middle finger pressed together, palm upwards).

Older dogs can be a little tricky to teach 'sit'. As you take the treat over their eyeline they take a step backwards. Try doing it with the dog standing in front of something so as he steps backwards, he bumps into the sofa - this usually sorts it. It is much harder training an adult dog to sit but thankfully the vast majority will already know it.

Practise the sit at kerbs, for having the lead on, for giving a chew or a special toy making this a prerequisite for anything the dog might get. This way they catch on quick.

Quick Overview

1. Stand in front of the dog. Engage his attention on the treat in your hand by showing him it or waving it around his nose.
2. Hold the treat slightly above his head going *slowly* over his eye line (towards his back).
3. As he follows the sight of the treat his bottom plops down.
4. Say 'sit' once, click (or say 'good dog'), then give the treat.

10.5 Down

Down is the next progression. Sit or kneel on the floor. Ask the dog to sit, don't treat it (as it might think it's finished and get up and walk away). Hold a handful of tasty bits up to the dog's nose – try and connect the nose to your hand by allowing the dog to sniff and nibble but not have. Slowly, keeping the nose connected this way take your hand down to the floor and pull it very slightly forwards. Hold your hand there; this is a time for patience. As soon as the dog flops down say 'down' once (don't shout or say it loudly, a dog's hearing is usually excellent). Click (or say 'good dog') and give the treat. Then repeat this straight away starting from the sit.

If you have tried this multiple times and he keeps standing up, try going slower with your hand movement and keeping it closer to your dog's chest. If this doesn't work sit down on the floor with your legs out in front of you. Make a slight bridge by raising your knees off the ground (creating a tunnel). Encourage your dog under the tunnel by teasing him with a handful of treats. As long as your knees are at the right height your dog will follow the treats into the tunnel and automatically lie down. Say 'down', click (or say 'good dog') and give one treat. Repeat a few times and then go back to doing it from the sit position as above.

It is worth noting here that some dogs get this exercise straight away while some need a little time and can take a few sessions to grasp what is needed to earn the treat. Don't be tempted to push down on the dog's back or to pull his front legs out from underneath him so he crashes to the floor (and don't let anyone else do it either). These are old fashioned methods, that in the worst case, could cause physical harm, and at best could make your dog unhappy about doing downs.

Once a dog has done this 5 - 10 times it is worth progressing on to the next stage. After all, you don't want to have to grovel on the floor with your dog when he is fourteen years old to get him to lie down. What we want is to be able to stand up, point to the floor and say 'down'. Getting there quickly is a good objective.

Now you want to be standing up and bending over instead of sitting or kneeling down. Holding several treats in your hand to make it interesting, make a point with your index finger (like shooting with a pretend gun). Bend over and glue the dog's nose to your hand as above. Go down most of the way stopping about two to three centimetres off the ground and hold that position while saying 'down' at the same time. Your dog should flop straight down. If he doesn't, stay where you are and don't be tempted to go all the way to the floor.

Thinking time for the dog is needed, as the signals you are giving are slightly different. Hold the position and only move or start again if your dog gets up and walks away. If your dog is finding this change difficult, take your hand down slower. Don't keep stopping and starting, pointing to the floor and repeating down. This just creates confusion and the dog's head just bobs up and down. Clear, slow, consistent signals are what we are aiming for. Don't forget to click and treat. You can repeat the down word once if you can't help yourself; but you don't have to.

The next time you do down (straight away would be good), hold your hand just a little higher – and so on and so forth – until you are standing and pointing to the floor. This process can be done in a few minutes but can also take several days/weeks of short training sessions.

Now start adding 'down' into your daily life and perhaps transpose some of the situations you would normally ask for a sit, to a down.

Quick Overview

1. Start in the sit position.
2. Using a handful of treats engage his attention on your hand by showing him them or waving them around his nose.
3. Slowly take your hand down to the floor, vertically, keeping his nose interested.
4. If he is not lying down yet *slowly* pull your hand away from him along the floor.
5. As he flops down, say 'down' once.
6. Click (or say 'good dog') and give one of the treats.

10.6 Stand

Stand is one of the easiest tasks to train for and also the one you are least likely to use. Typically stand is used when grooming a dog or when at the vets checking limbs and joints. But it is useful to know, particularly for the veterinary situation where the dog can already be under some emotional pressure and pulling it around to force it to stand up can increase the stress.

Start in the sit position (that's the dog, not you). Hold a treat to the dog's nose and pull it away, horizontally in line with the dog's nose, very slowly. As the dog follows the treat, it automatically stands up, so say 'stand' at the same time. Click (or say 'good dog') and give the treat. Make sure you don't pull the treat upwards at all – as this is the sit signal and will cause confusion.

Some dogs will bum-shuffle along the floor or lie down. Don't stop. Keep pulling the treat slowly (and horizontally) away. After a few seconds of cleaning the floor with its bottom, or crawling along on its belly, the dog will stand. If you do stop and start again you will have to go through the whole bum-shuffling sequence again.

The hand signal for stand can then be introduced once you have repeated it a few times. Hold a treat between your index and middle finger. Keep your palm flat and palm side towards the dog (engaging the nose with the treat). Slowly pull your hand away and say stand. As he stands, click and give the treat. Your hand signal then becomes a flat palm pulled away from the dog. Simple!

Quick Overview

1. Start with your dog in the sit position.
2. Hold a handful of treats up to his nose.
3. *Slowly*, pull your hand horizontally away from your dog in line with his nose.
4. As he stands, say 'Stand' once.
5. Click (or say 'good dog') and then give one of the treats.

10.7 Walking on a Loose Lead

This objective should be taken as a work in progress with young dogs (and some older dogs!!) and requires persistence, consistency and oodles of patience. Dogs like to get where they are going quickly, especially if it's the park. Putting a lead on stops them from going at the pace they want to, so they pull against it. We automatically pull back, they pull harder and hey presto we have successfully taught our dog to pull on the lead.

Try and think differently about the lead. See it as a safety cord, rope or chain, not as something we use to control the dog. The lead is there to stop the dog running off and doing something stupid. You control the dog using food, treats, a toy, your magnetic personality – encouraging him to follow you and creating *the habit* of following you. Sounds simple – but simple it is not!

I am right-handed so I'm going to explain this for the right-handed person. If you are left-handed or have a weakness on one side, then walk the dog on whichever side is more comfortable for you.

Hold the lead in your left hand. KEEP YOUR LEFT ARM RELAXED (shake it out if you need to). Shorten the lead so the dog can only take one step away from you maximum. We don't want to give him too many options because he'll take them. Put the clicker in your lead hand if you are using one. Have a treat bag on (or bum bag, similar to a treat bag but clips around your waist) so you can get at your treats easily. Have a handful of treats in your right hand and hold this hand across your body so it sticks out just above your left hip. Engage the dog's nose with the treats and if needed waggle your hand about as you move forwards *at a normal pace*. Try and walk at a regular speed. I don't know why, but many people walk at a snail's pace when doing heel and this is very boring for a dog.

After two or three steps say 'heel', click (or say 'good dog') and treat. Repeat this a few times and once your dog starts to get the idea say 'heel', click (or say 'good dog') and treat perhaps every five or six paces. Once this is starting to get some consistency, say 'heel' and click (or say 'good dog') every eight or nine paces, but perhaps only treat every two or three clicks. Otherwise, you can get through a bag of treats just getting up the drive.

As your dog becomes competent at this, reduce the clicks and treats. This can take many weeks/months.

If your dog pulls, stop dead. If your lead arm is rigid and tense you will tolerate a huge amount of pulling before you do anything about it, so make sure it is relaxed. It can then act as a barometer - as soon as your arm goes up past 45 degrees stop dead. Engage the nose again, and take two to three steps backwards, bringing the dog back into your side, do not treat or praise. Then start again. This is where the frustration kicks in for both dog and owner as you repeat ad nauseum (until you want to scream).

Try and stay calm and relaxed.

It is very important that your lead arm is relaxed and down at your side in a normal position, so you know when to stop dead. By stepping two to three paces back your whole body then takes the strain of bringing the dog back at your side – not just your arm. This allows anyone of any build to use this method, not just body builders!

Practise heel in the garden and around the house (or in any secure area) without using a lead but following all the steps above as if a lead is attached. This is the best way to practise walking on a loose lead. Then you just add the lead in after.

For dogs that have learned to pull on the lead it is often necessary to use a training aid such as a head collar or harness. Please do not view this as a failure on your part or that your dog is faulty in some way. Most young dogs pull. They are simply excited and eager. These training aids take the pull out of the dog giving you the right circumstances to then train him as above. It is difficult in the extreme to lead-train a dog that is fighting against you all the way, but it can give you Popeye muscles if you are partial to that look! It's not forever either. I advise many people to walk the dog out on an aid of some description and once it has had a run around walk back on his collar. This can work well as a compromise. And for us women, with limited upper body strength, it can make the difference between us walking the dog or not walking him (or grabbing every lamp post on the way to the park to reduce our speed!)

And sticking a choke (codename check) chain, noose (codename slip lead), pinch or prong (sticking spikes into your dog's neck) collar or any other such instrument of torture on the dog is completely unnecessary and rather cruel.

As for which kit to use, that is a tricky question. One method of determining what to go for is if the dog is pulling all the time, go for a head collar (like a Gentle Leader). If he is pulling some of the time, then try a harness. The harness should be one where the lead clips onto a ring at the dog's chest which corrects pulling (like an Easy Walk), not a basic body harness (clips on in the middle of the back) as these encourage the dog to pull harder and may cause muscle loss on the back legs as the front end builds to almost Staffie proportions. Obviously if the dog *really objects* to a head collar (they all object a bit), then go straight to a pull correcting harness.

Whichever kit you choose, it should ultimately fit easily, be comfortable for the dog (not cause chafing etc) and make walking easier and more enjoyable for both of you. You may have to try a range of walking aids before you find what is right for you and your dog.

If you think about it in terms how a dog is built and the relative delicateness of the neck area, a collar is possibly the worst place to try and control the beastie. Long term you could be looking at neck damage, muscle build-up in all the wrong places and throat problems. Any of these can occur if the dog is constantly pulling on a collar, and if he's coughing or gagging while walking, change to a correcting device straight away.

Quick Overview

1. Hold the lead in your hand that is next to the dog. Put the clicker in this hand (if using one). Keep your lead arm relaxed.
2. In your other hand have some nice smelly treats.
3. Hold your treat hand across your body so it sits by your waist or just above your hip.
4. Wiggle your treat hand to get your dog's attention.
5. Start walking at normal pace.
6. Say 'heel', click (or say 'good dog') if he is following your hand and release a treat.
7. Aim to increase the number of steps between each click and treat.
8. Alternatively, don't reward each click. Try every two or three clicks for every treat and keep expanding this.
9. If your lead arm goes above 45 degrees stop dead, take three paces back to bring dog back in at your side, and continue walking. No 'good dog', no click!

10.8 Coming When Called

Dogs need to learn to come when called (commonly referred to as recall) in a variety of situations, for example at the end of a walk. They have to be called away from other dogs or people they find interesting, just as they have to be called in from the garden, or after escaping out of the front door after a cat. Teaching the dog to come when called is one of the main reasons people attend training classes.

Ideally the training should begin with a puppy around the house and garden before he's even allowed out. Letting a puppy off the lead in a field or park at twelve to fourteen weeks (as soon as they have had their vaccinations) is a scary prospect – but in fact it's the best time. They are very dependent upon you just now. Waiting until the puppy is six months old, a teenager, knowing where he is and how to get home, reduces the likelihood he will return to you, or even care where you are. If a dog of any age has a problem returning when called, then you'll need to re-train from scratch.

Firstly, we want them to respond quickly to the sound of their name. This can be achieved by calling the dog's name when he is nearby, and rewarding him with praise or a treat when he looks round at you. The name is the attention getter! Then we have to teach them another word that means 'come back'. Words like 'come' are poor – dogs always respond better to two syllables, like 'come here'. ('Here!' is the signal I use, but I pronounce it 'hee-yah'. Common I know.) In the house, walk past your dog and call him – 'Cricket, come here!' – keep *walking away* from him. Offer big praise, a food treat, or a quick game the instant he catches up with you, but not until you have slipped your fingers gently into his collar. If you're using a clicker, this is the time to click, and then give a 'sweetie'. Do this off and on throughout the day, around the house and garden (repeating this over and over will often bore a dog – try not to overdo it).

Sliding fingers into the collar ensures your dog doesn't come, grab the reward and scoot – because he has then had the treat and is still free to do as he pleases. Never grab the collar as a dog can quickly learn to duck out of the way. Simply slide your hand underneath the collar by the ear or under the chin. Going over the head can be a bit scary for a dog.

Walking away is very important. If you call your dog and stand still, he may look, decide he knows where you are and continue what he is doing. If you call your dog, and then walk towards him, you are undoing your training and the dog reads the situation as he hears the command, meaning we are coming for him. This can lead to a lovely game of chase. Lovely for the dog, not for us!

Once a dog starts coming when you call him (which could take a few minutes, hours or days), we need to change the number of times we give him a sweetie for doing it. Dogs like to gamble. A dog can make a decision, as we pay witness to each day. 'Shall I steal the steak off the kitchen table?' he wonders, nose twitching and scanning for goodies. He decides quickly, depending on the value of the prize and how easy it is to steal. Even dogs previously caught pilfering will check where we are and do a swift risk-assessment.

The basic factors in their decision-making are 'where's the loot?' and 'what risk is there in getting it?'

This is no different to the dog who, upon hearing his owner calling him, weighs up his options, turns tail, and runs off in the opposite direction. Some even look back as if to say, 'not likely, not yet!' The poor owner is left stranded, with no option but to shout, stamp his feet, wave his lead in the air and blow on his whistle. All good frustration outlets, but they don't get the dog back. Telling the dog off when he finally does return can reduce your frustration, making you feel temporarily better. But all it teaches the dog is that 'come here' really means 'come here and be punished!' ensuring the dog is even more reluctant to come back next time.

What we need to do is stack the odds in our favour. Make the choice easy. We hold the reward, and it is one worth having, but it is only available if the dog returns quickly. However, giving a reward every time a dog comes back to us starts it thinking. 'Do I want the biscuit, or shall I go and sniff in those bushes?' It's better to mix rewards with praise – we should always be happy to see them – and perhaps offer some dog food for a reasonable return but give them a very special treat for turning on a sixpence and racing back at full speed (remembering to put the brakes on, of course).

The special 'come here' treat must be something the dog prizes above everything else. It needs to be changed frequently, to keep the dog really interested. Showing the dog the reward before you allow him off the lead hones his senses as to what he could earn. Dogs understand the rules of a game swiftly, and the 'come here' game can be taught in a couple of sessions in the garden or on an extender lead, using a multitude of rewards with a differing range of values. With some, a squeaky toy can be that highly regarded prize.

Quick Overview

1. Walking away from your dog, call his name and use your selected recall signal (such as 'come here' or 'what's this').
2. As the nosey devil follows you, click (or say 'good dog') and give him a treat.
3. Slide your fingers into his collar as you treat (good habit to make sure you actually have hold of him as you reward).
4. Use this command or signal often, always coupled with a treat, praise or a toy to make it fun, to create the habit of coming when called.

10.9 Coming Back Issues

Problems with coming back are numerous. Some dogs go completely deaf momentarily, while others can glance in your direction acknowledging they have heard, but still refuse to return. The teasing types come in close, and then dart just out of reach. These have often learned to do this through being grabbed. Hunting dogs become so involved in the eye, stalk, chase, pounce, bite, kill routine that nothing else matters once they have caught a scent. The desire to be chased spurs some dogs on. As you take a step towards them, they run off. These dogs have often been taught this in the back garden – you chasing your dog for fun – and then transpose the game to the field. Playing with other dogs can be great, while returning to you may be a bit boring. The dog that is only called in at the end of the walk may decide it's not yet time. When being trained to 'come here' using food, some dogs quickly learn to grab the grub, and then scoot off – very clever and doubly rewarding. The stubborn amongst them may just stay where they are, and insist you go and fetch them!

Starting 'come here' from the beginning and keeping them on an extender lead or long line in the meantime is a sensible way forward. Each time your dog ignores you when you call him, the pleasure of being free motivates him to do it again. Dogs who take the food and run need to be taught that they only get the food once the lead is on or you have hold of their collar. This can be quickly achieved by holding the food tightly in your hand, allowing the dog to sniff and lick at it, and releasing it slowly. While the dog is concentrating on the food hand, slip the other hand through the collar. Once you have a good grip of the collar then release the rest of the food. Keep hold of the dog and make a fuss of him. Ask him to sit. Once he has sat tell him to 'Go play'. At this point let go of the collar. Many dogs see the lead being unclipped as a sign to run off, but if you always get the dog to sit, hold his collar, and then tell him to 'Go play', the dog learns that he cannot go until you say so. This avoids the problem of having to fight with the dog to get the lead off.

10.10 *Hide and Seek*

This is a great game to play with your dog on walks. As he is sniffing at a tree or burying his nose in a bush, vanish quietly behind something and keep silent (you must keep very quiet, or your dog will suss out where you are using his ears and may not feel the need to seek you out). Wait for him to come and find you. When he does find you, throw a party – give him a sweetie and loads of fuss. This game makes your dog use his nose to find you, something dogs like to do. It also teaches him to keep an eye on where you are – to continually check you are still around.

This can be a good game to play if your dog's recall is a bit hit and miss. By disappearing suddenly, you can 'shock' your dog into keeping an eye on where you are and paying a bit more attention.

10.11 *Stopping Jumping Up*

It's true that little puppies are cute, and people tend to encourage them to jump up. But they grow, and some grow very quickly and can begin to hurt people quite early on. So, this behaviour does need to be nipped in the bud quickly, ideally when the dog is a puppy or adolescent, before a real habit is formed.

Dogs jump up at people to get attention and it usually works. Even if that attention is 'ouch', or 'Buster stop' screamed loudly while the dog is pushed off. There are several methods that I find work well for this problem and a combination of them used in different situations can quickly stop this from becoming a major issue.

When meeting people out in the street, or visitors to your house, immediately when the dog goes to jump up at them, pull back on the lead, harness or collar and say 'No'. Then give your sit command. When sitting (or standing) slip your fingers into his collar or harness and apply slight downward pressure so the dog can then be fussed by the person he was trying to jump on without the risk of him jumping up and head butting. If he goes to jump up again, pull back, say 'No' and then 'sit' (don't be tempted to give treats for this or tell your dog it is good as your dog will learn to jump up, in order to be told to get off, and then sit for a reward – 1.5 and 1.13 – 1.15). The compromise for behaving nicely is the attention from the person he wants it from i.e., the visitor. Be consistent with this – no attention unless paws are on the ground – and your dog will quickly give up jumping at people.

When your dog jumps up at you or other household members because you have been out for a while and the dog is over-excited, a different approach may work better. There are a few options for this. Choose whichever suits you best and apply it for many weeks / months consistently.

Option 1. Ignore your dog when you get home. Your dog is looking for attention, which is fine. It's just the method he is employing that is annoying. Ignore him completely (don't look at him, talk to him, touch him) so the jumping up strategy does not work in getting the dog what he wants. Eventually he should stop and look to other ways to say hello. The downside to this method is that he will try harder, so you do have to be prepared to go through an escalation of the jumping (maybe a little nipping or grabbing at clothes) for him to finally give it up and try something else. This escalation could take hours, days, weeks, months – depending on how sure the dog is in his own mind that jumping up is the way to go. You just have to be prepared to go through that. This works well for some people.

Another downside to this method is that your dog may be very sensitive and feel he is in trouble or that you are upset with him as you are ignoring him. This can in some cases cause some anxiety in the dog and he may pee or poo when he is left or start chewing things he never has before. If you see these side effects, stop this method immediately.

Option 2. An alternative to this is asking for a simple sit. Keep a treat or special toy in your pocket or in the porch. As you walk through the door say a calm 'hello' and give your hand signal and word for sit. Wait patiently, maybe waving the treat around gently to focus his attention on it. Once he sits, maybe then ask for a down (hand signal plus word). Give the treat and a calm stroke and he should be calm enough not to jump. Sit and down are often used by trainers and behaviourists as a calming position. Try this method for six weeks to two months – he should come and sit automatically after this time if everyone does the same (if the dog is still jumping up at one or two individuals and not at the rest of the household then their consistency should be improved).

Option 3. Another fun way of stopping this type of jumping up is to keep a nice toy (perhaps a squeaky) in the porch or on the doorstep. As you walk through the door give it a couple of squeaks and then throw it. Many dogs will go after the toy and then trot around with it wagging furiously. If the dog catches on to this one, he may then automatically go and grab a toy when you come through the door. Simple, easy and very little effort needed. There are no downsides to this approach that I have found to date – other than with the dog that doesn't value toys!

> ***Option 4.*** Do ballroom dancing. Without looking at the dog step away so he falls to the floor. Keep calm and relaxed. As he comes from the right side, step left. As he comes from the front, step back etc. This is a very calm, passive approach and the dog simply keeps falling to the floor and gains no attention whatsoever. I love this method as it is stress free for all and does feel like ballroom dancing!

For the dog that starts jumping up at random (and possibly nipping or grabbing at clothing), we need to be quite firm. The randomness of this is what causes most difficulties as a dog can easily catch you off balance and knock you over – he doesn't need to be particularly big. Yes, he wants attention, but we really shouldn't give him any for this – he will never stop otherwise. I find a time-out works really well (1.11 – 1.15). Simply say 'No' and get hold of his collar and carry or walk him to the porch, downstairs toilet or to the back door and put him out of the way for two minutes. You don't usually need longer than this, but if he comes back in all lairy do it for a little bit longer. It's a calm-down session for him and is quite a strong punishment as he is being excluded from the family. Don't shout or get angry – just say 'No' and eject him quickly. When he is allowed out again ignore him for 30 seconds and then act as though nothing has happened. If he starts his crazy behaviour again, repeat this process. Consistency in this approach should stop this behaviour in a few weeks. Don't forget to ignore him for 30 seconds when you open the door, so you don't reward him by mistake.

10.12 Teaching Your Dog to Leave

Getting a dog of any age to leave is very important, and I'm not just talking about getting him to drop your new iPhone either. There are many things around the house, garden and especially out on walks that will attract a puppy or adult dog that could be potentially harmful, even deadly. Teaching leave in a harsh way by yanking items off them or physically pulling the dog away can encourage the dog to run away from you or worse still, swallow what they have or become aggressive. Leave needs to be taught properly and gently in order for it to have the long-term benefits you can achieve.

You can start this, as with any training, at any age. But it is always easier if you do it sooner rather than later.

Take two handfuls of the puppy's or dog's food. Kneel down on the floor. Don't give the dog any command like sit or down. Place a piece of food on the floor and say 'leave it' gently (you can use leave, but the two syllables in 'leave it' tends to give a quicker and stronger response). As the dog goes for the food, push him away (not aggressively) using the same hand and as you do, pop a piece of food in his mouth. I find that pushing the food into his mouth works best, so you are basically pushing against his muzzle. Immediately put another piece of food on the floor again saying, 'leave it' and push away using the food and popping one piece in his mouth. Continue with this (reloading from your other hand) until all the food is gone. Pick up the pile on the floor and start again.

Of course, we want all this to be gentle and nice, but it may be a bit of a scramble in the beginning, and you might have to fend off the beast using the other arm as a block for the first few goes. Don't get harsh or be tempted to get cross. Once the dog sits back, watching and waiting for his treat, leaving the ever-increasing pile on the floor, then only reward for this and push back giving no treat if he comes forward when you put food down and say, 'leave it'. Then we can progress this immediately by putting two or three bits down to everyone the dog gets (increasing all the while until you can dump a pile of food on the floor and give just one piece in reward for leaving it).

Once you can do this easily (and it might take a few meals given like this over a week) then we are ready to move on.

Take something tasty, like a pig's ear or juicy bone and place it on the floor. Put your dog's lead on – very important. Walk him up to the item keeping the lead shortish so he can't just make a grab for the treat. Hold him there, about ten centimetres away. Don't yank on the lead or let him touch or lick the item. Gently say 'leave it' repeatedly until he turns away from the tasty item. Immediately click or say 'good dog' but reward about 8 metres away so he learns to leave and come right away from something. Walk him up and repeat what you have just done, remembering not to yank at all on the lead. Only repeat this once or twice. You are now ready to take this exercise out on your walks.

Practising leave on walks is really important. This is the time you need this the most and there are always plenty of things to practise with. As you are walking up the street or in the park and your dog shows interest in some rubbish, a poo etc., hold him there like you did at home and repeat 'leave it' to him, remembering not to shout or to yank on the lead. Click or praise when he finally comes away voluntarily, walk away and reward eight plus metres away.

The reasons for not shouting I have already given, but why not a yank down the lead – surely he will learn quicker?

Yes, your dog will learn more swiftly, but it is dependent upon him being on the lead. A dog doesn't really need to learn leave on the lead as we can always just pull him away. What we want is for him to learn to leave stuff when he is *off the lead*, so we cannot use the lead as part of the signalling process. It must be entirely voluntary from the dog. This is crucial in terms of getting a decent leave from a loose dog.

With this exercise the more practise you do out on your walks, the more proficient he will get and if he gets bored of it – great! He will stop going for stuff, which is what we want in the long run. Don't set him up with items at home – you'll be wasting your time as dogs catch on quick that they can't have it, so learn nothing new, or they learn to go for it in order to be told to leave it to earn a treat which is not what we are looking for. It is important to only practise this on your walks with real life rubbish, which is different and in a different place each time, the side effect is learning to ignore stuff – the ideal outcome.

Quick Overview

1. Have food in both hands. Put a piece down and with the same hand push the dog away and pop food in his mouth. Repeat until the dog doesn't move forward when you put the food down. Then you only reward that.
2. If the dog does come forward when you put the food down after this, gently push away with no food. Only reward for putting it on the floor and the dog not making any moves.
3. Repeat until you can put lots of food down saying 'leave it' each time you do.
4. Take your practise out on a walk. For every unsavoury item he expresses interest in, stand still, repeat 'leave it' in a happy voice until he voluntarily comes away, walk away praising and treat eight ish metres away.

10.13 Stay

Stay means 'do nothing while I go away and come back'. That's what we want the dog to learn. This exercise is very useful.

To begin with simply ask your dog to sit in front of you. Don't reward the sit. Then try and turn around on the spot in front of him. If he is still sitting, click (or say 'good dog') and give him a treat. If not, try again. If he really won't sit for a full turn, try a half turn remembering to take your face away, and build it up to a full turn. Once you have mastered the full turn add in the word 'Stay'. Using a flat hand for your hand signal (almost like you are going to pat him on the head, without being that close). Give the hand signal and word at the same time and turn around on the spot again. Once you have done this a few times, remembering to reward each time, then start turning and taking one step away.

Ask your dog to sit using the word and hand signal. Then stay, again using the word and hand signal. Turn your back on him and take one step away as normally as possible (don't start walking funny and acting all stiff as this can unsettle the dog). Turn to him and go back. Click (or say 'good dog') and reward him straight away. Repeat this and try and add in an extra step away each time if you can, without him getting up to follow you. If he does start getting up, you may have to do three steps away several times until he's got it then move on to four steps. Then all you need to do is gradually increase the time and distance away.

There are four rules to stick to in order for your stay to be reliable.

1. Never call his name while you are away from him. If you want to remind him to stay, just say 'stay'. Saying 'Max stay' may induce him to come to you. Some people think the dog should be looking at them when doing a stay and call the name to get the attention, swiftly undoing all their hard work. Personally, I am happy if the dog is looking around, as long as he is staying (thumb up, bum and brain in neutral is what we really want – that indicates a nice, relaxed stay, which can then be used in daily life).

2. Never call him to you – always go back and reward him for staying put. If you start calling him to you, the stay will become unreliable, as the dog will interpret the slightest signal from you to be 'come'. Scratching your nose for example or raising an eyebrow could set the dog off on a mad scramble to come and get the treat, and this is definitely not a relaxed calm stay. Always, always, always go back, stand in front of him and then click (or say 'good dog') and reward.

3. Don't be tempted to walk backwards. Your dog has to learn to behave in a stay even if your back is to him (which is why we do the turning around bit at the beginning). If your dog can only stay put while you are facing him – then he can't do a stay. Let's face it – teaching him by walking backwards doesn't really give you a usable task unless you go round walking backwards in your regular life. And you might just fall over something...

4. If your dog sits up, lies down or stands up while doing a stay, but does not move off the spot you can still reward him. Simply put him back into the original position first and then click (or say 'good dog') and treat.

Practising stay is boring for a dog. Vary where you practise and what you are doing as you walk away; maybe putting the kettle on, getting the dog a treat out of the cupboard etc. Only do a handful of stays several times a day, some in the kitchen, some in the garden, some out on walks, as your dog might get bored and not want to play that game.

10.14 Fetch

Getting a dog to bring a toy back and release it is easier if you use two toys that are exactly the same. Throw the first one just a short distance from you and allow time for the dog to pick it up. Once it is in the dog's mouth, call him to you. When he is near, bring the other toy out from behind your back and tease him with it or bounce it on the floor. This makes him drop the first toy. Immediately throw the second toy as his reward. As he gets good at releasing the toy, begin saying 'drop it'.

Once he is leaving the article on these words alone, you no longer need the two toys. You can use treats, waving them under his nose to encourage him to release the toy, but we want the game to be self-sustaining, and as you are essentially rewarding him for dropping, the dog starts dropping earlier and earlier and not bringing it back to you so using two toys achieves this for us and gives a much better result. The toys have to be the same, or the dog will favour one over the other.

10.15 Wait

Once you have a reliable stay and your dog has been performing this in many different places you can start with wait (you need a good, solid stay before you start working on this one, or you may lose your stay – so be patient).

Wait should be thought of as pause, pay attention, a command is coming. The most common use of wait is when it is followed by 'come here'. For instance, asking your dog to sit and wait at the front door, you step through, and then call your dog through. Wait has many, many applications on and off the lead, and is well worth training for.

Start with a sit at the side of you. Give the stay hand signal but use the word 'wait' instead of 'stay'. Take two steps forward and then call your dog in to the side of you and into sit. Click or say, 'good dog' and reward. Increase the distance between you each time by one or two steps. Then you can start using wait. Use it at kerbs, asking your dog to sit and wait, then come as you cross the road. Getting out of the car – open the boot or door immediately giving the hand signal and the word 'wait', then call him out of the car. Using wait at doors in and out of the house gets this exciting situation under some control. Off-lead in the park you may be coming up to a corner, give the signal 'wait' as you check all is good, then perhaps something like 'on you go', to say he can move again.

Wait is simply a pause, followed by another command, and for this reason it is one that can be practised a lot in many different situations without the dog switching off.

Printed in Great Britain
by Amazon

63348352R00102